SOOTHING THE
BEAST WITHIN

Curious
Open
Accepting
Loving.

SOOTHING THE BEAST WITHIN

A LOVING PATH TO END FOOD ADDICTION

By

Nancy Routley

Order this book online at www.trafford.com
or email orders@trafford.com

Most Trafford titles are also available at major online book retailers.

Printed in the United States of America.

ISBN: 978-1-4669-0743-0 (sc)
ISBN: 978-1-4669-0744-7 (hc)
ISBN: 978-1-4669-0745-4 (e)

Library of Congress Control Number: 2011962217

Trafford rev. 01/04/2012

 www.trafford.com

North America & international
toll-free: 1 888 232 4444 (USA & Canada)
phone: 250 383 6864 ♦ fax: 812 355 4082

Table of Contents

For Sue

Who taught me so much more than I ever realized.

Certainly grief fed the beast, and with her encroaching middle age came more and greater opportunities for it. Every passage, but particularly the corporeal kind, further embellish Mary Gooch. Thirty pounds for her mother, accumulated over many months, years ago, although Irma was not actually deceased. The lost babies, so long ago, had added fifteen and twenty pounds respectively. Then it was the ten when her father died in the spring. And another ten with her cat Mr. Barkley in the summer.[1]

Adapted from The Wife's Tale—Lori Lansens

INTRODUCTION

LOSING WEIGHT IS like spring pruning; the shrub is trimmed to half of its former size only to double its blossoms by the end of the summer. And yet we don't learn—we repeat the process again and again. We buy magazines that promise the ultimate answers, join too many weight loss programs to remember, retreat to 'spas'. Anything to lose that dreaded fat. This quest is all-consuming and often overwhelming. And it is an obsession that has become the norm in many developed nations.

Nevertheless, despite the claims of the $30 billion diet industry, dieting does not work for the majority of us. Dieting actually makes us fat. **Up to 90 percent of us who try to lose weight by dieting, fail.**[1] We put it back on within a year, often gaining more weight than was originally lost. Low carb diets, high protein diets, diets based on food combining, or blood types—although there may be science to support these programs, they are rarely sustainable.

When the prescription is followed to the letter, success might be achieved, but most dieters are unable to maintain the necessary vigilance.

The list below is a sampling of the theories posited as explanations for the increased rates of obesity:

> Unprecedented amounts of accessible, inexpensive foods at our fingertips.
> An increased sedentary population resulting from our dependence upon motorized transportation and an inordinate amount of time spent sitting in front of electronic devices, to name a few.
> Physical education programs eliminated in many schools.
> A shifting acceptance of obesity among some groups, seen as a sign of power or of pride of one's 'big booty'.
> A lack of nutritional understanding.
> An increased fascination with food, evident in the number of restaurants, cooking shows and all things food related.
> A normalization of eating out and/or ordering in.
> An acceptance of eating between meals, often seen as necessary.
> Snacking during the evening—a habit often thought to be normal.
> Food is used for celebration, reward and connection way beyond special occasions.
> Less available time for preparing healthy meals and an increase in relying on pre-made, packaged and processed food.

> Typical daily food intake and portion sizes have increased dramatically.

It would be remiss of me to 'pooh pooh' these ideas as having no validity. Of course what you eat in terms of quantity and quality affects the number on the scale. How active you are also plays a role. Obviously we are affected by the starring role food plays in our society.

Yet the weight loss industry focuses almost solely on diet and exercise as the solution to weight management. If we eat right and exercise, (what exactly that means continues to be hotly debated), we will have this problem licked, despite what is happening in our greater society. So, why are we still fat?

Lucy is a slim woman who works in the cubical next to you. Every day she walks by the same gauntlet of restaurants loaded with delicious, tempting smells and tastes as you do. She enjoys food, never diets and seems to eat whatever she wants. She takes a train to work from the suburbs and exercises only moderately. Despite this, Lucy does not struggle with weight issues. What is the reason? Luck? Genetics?

The heart of the matter, the truth of why so many of us carry extra weight is that food has become a way to cope with life's stresses, a way to manage emotions. Because of the sheer abundance and availability of food in our society, we now have a simple way to shove down our anxieties and manage any negative feeling that threatens to come up.

Yet there are still few voices in the weight loss industry that speak to this reality. There are few discussions regarding the emotional and spiritual aspects of our weight struggles. There is still little dialogue about our fears and how we manage them. Too often, our sorrows, worries and pain lie hidden. It's like acquiring a garden patch, tilling the soil, buying some seed and carefully sowing them. But, where's the water? We can't figure out why nothing is growing. It's obvious, yet we missed it. Like cultivating a successful garden, we have to attend to each aspect of the self (the mind, body and spirit) in order to permanently end our weight battle.

We lose the weight, receive compliments, tell ourselves it's for good this time, buy those new jeans, but before long the jeans get tighter and our inner monologues start up, the ones that made us overeat in the first place. We slip back into our old ways. The pressures of life—stresses, dramas, sometimes benign, sometimes truly traumatic events—lead us back to our familiar eating patterns, back to using food for comfort. We start stuffing ourselves in secret. We start making excuses: "It's not my fault, its genetic. I can't help it, who can eat that way? It's too hard to find the right foods. It is too much work creating these meals. The whole thing is ridiculous. Just accept the extra weight, forget it!"

Soon we are bingeing again. Off to the fridge we go, searching, looking for something. Nothing in there, into the cupboards, ahh, chocolate chips, okay I'll just make some cookies for the kids—they love cookies—get out the butter, flour, sugar, pecans and chocolate chips, a few chips and pecans for the mouth, some into the measuring cup. Back into the fridge for the eggs, spy the leftover lasagna, kind of gross but why not? Eat half of it cold—close to lunch, may as well have lunch. Slip the rest of the lasagna into the microwave while creaming the butter with the sugar. As the lunch heats, munch a few more chocolate chips, follow with a pecan chaser, then a quick lick of the cookie dough. Get a piece of that old crusty bread to have with the lasagna, a little stale but if sliced thin and toasted, it will be fine. A generous slather of butter, eat a few pieces while the lasagna goes in for another minute. Finish the first of the toast then pop in two more pieces while waiting and grab a couple chocolate chips before dumping them into the batter. Starting to feel full. The microwave dings. Let the lasagna rest for a minute, finish forming the cookies, slip the first batch in the oven and sit down like a civilized person to finish the lasagna and two more slices of toast. Take the dishes to the sink.

The shame sneaks in.

I am such a loser. I have no willpower at all. I'm going to be fat for the rest of my life. I'm so weak. No, stop! You just overate a little today but after the cookies are done you can have just one later with a cup of tea and then for dinner you will eat only vegetables. You can do this—it's a good plan.

A piece of cookie breaks off as it slides from the pan. I should have waited until they were cool, but I never do and they always fall apart. Just eat that one piece that broke off. Hot! Burns tongue. Wait until they cool. Good job, pick a nice big one, after all, it will be the only one, put it on a pretty plate and sit down and enjoy it, slowly. Delicious. Perfectly reasonable and totally in control. Get up and get the next pan out of the oven. Again, start taking them off while they are hot. Two more cookies crack in half. Better eat the broken pieces, ruins the look of the platter.

I'm disgusting! I feel sick … these pants were loose last week. Stop it, just stop it! Get out of the kitchen, go to your room read a book.

In the bedroom, door shut, trying to concentrate on the novel, but the cookies are taking over my thoughts. Just one more. Quickly dash down stairs, get a plate, remember there's some vanilla ice cream left in the freezer, empty the carton by putting it on the cookie. Fantastic. Quickly shove the empty ice cream carton to the bottom of the garbage can and sneak upstairs to savor my treat while nestled in bed.

The neighbor calls—she has made a big shepherd's pie and apple crumble. Do we all want to come over for dinner? Absolutely! We'll bring the bread and wine.

There's always tomorrow.

*   *   *

Soothing the Beast Within: A Loving Path to End Food Addiction explains what emotional eating is, provides ways to uncover the reasons beneath the behavior and offers solutions for change. This book will provide tips to help you become more present in your life, more mindful; the elusive yet attainable ability to be in attendance and present in any given moment, instead of thinking about what just happened or what is going to happen. The techniques teach you specific ways to pause and reflect so you can see your own behavior, feel your emotions and make conscious choices. This book provides a path to change your relationship with food into a healthy love affair, one that nourishes your body, strengthens your spirit and feeds your soul. Wherever you are on your weight loss quest, understand that this book is not about getting skinny; it is about being the healthiest you. The images we are bombarded with in the media, the movie stars, sports celebrities and models are not realistic. They are ridiculous standards that most of us can't and should not want to achieve.

Your doctor can suggest a healthy weight for your frame. You can also look up body weight standards, including BMI (body mass index) charts, online. Your goal weight may fall between the suggested guidelines or you may reach the outer edges and beyond. My goal weight falls in the high range of healthy, bordering on overweight, but I take these standards with a grain of salt. I know what feels and looks right on me. When my weight is lower, like many women of a certain age, I lose my face, my breasts shrink and my butt fades away. Not the healthy, vibrant look I'm going for!

Don't fixate on what the scales say. We have done that for too long and it makes us miserable; BMI is a more important number than poundage because a high percentage of body fat is associated with an increased risk of disease. Work toward being the best you and remember, your body may never be your ideal of thin. I encourage you to make peace with that.[2] Making peace with your body means accepting what you can't change, and learning to love yourself despite the fact that your legs are short and your butt is flat. Making peace does not mean we don't strive for change, it can actually do the opposite; it gives us the energy for change.

If you are younger than me and are ready to hear this message, congratulate yourself for getting off the diet roller coaster early. It's time for us, men and women, to stop loathing our bodies, learn to love ourselves and make peace with food. That is what will make us thinner.

MY STORY

My unsuccessful attempts at weight loss focused almost solely on the latest diet craze. I went on my first diet when I was fourteen. Being considerably taller than my cute, tiny girlfriends, at five-foot-eight and 130 pounds, I decided I was fat. I wasn't. But I couldn't relate to the images in Seventeen Magazine. Those 'seventies' girls had long, blonde hair, sun-kissed noses and perfect teeth. I wanted to look just like they did. My face wasn't too bad, I just needed to be skinnier—that would fix everything. Thus started twenty-five years of yo-yo dieting, at the end of which I was at an all-time high of 180 pounds. I am sure that number would have climbed higher if it were not for my need and love of exercise I discovered in my early thirties. And I am convinced that if I had never dieted, age and genetics would have led me to top out around 145 pounds. Ah, but that is not the road I took.

At a conservative estimate, I went on a minimum of ten diets a year for at least twenty-five years. That is over 250 diets in my lifetime. It could easily be 300. By the age of forty, I had been a therapist for about five years, and it began to dawn on me that my unsuccessful quest for permanent weight loss might be about more than diet and exercise. Something else was going on. I looked for answers, but found few in weight-loss circles.

As a therapist, I work with people with addictions. Addictions are rampant in our society, showing up in numerous forms, from the obvious to the well-hidden. We can distinguish behaviors such as serious drug addiction—we see it on the streets of our cities. Sooner or later we realize that Aunt Mae isn't tired all the time, she's drunk. But less obvious behaviors, such as repeatedly choosing unhealthy partners, may not be recognized as an addiction to drama. It may be dismissed as bad luck.

As I worked with clients to help them understand what motivated their behavior and how to stop the destruction, I saw myself sitting there, offering support, empathy and suggestions, there was a voice in my head that grew increasingly louder, one I could no longer ignore. It was telling me that there was a lesson in this for me, too. Wasn't this the way I was with food?

The following is a typical scenario: By Thursday afternoon, I had spent the last three days working with women who had experienced abuse, or were still in abusive relationships. Stories, so many stories, some of triumph, many of extreme trauma. Once I got home, I headed to the fridge even before I removed my coat, and started shoving something in my mouth, all the while telling myself I was hungry. Yes, I was physiologically hungry, but the first piece of bread with peanut butter would have sufficed until dinnertime. But I didn't stop and I didn't notice—I was using food in an attempt to push down the emotional residue from my day. I was attempting to swallow my feelings.

A thought occurred to me. Was I addicted too? Surely not, I was in a helping profession. I knew the signs. How could I be addicted? I was a successful, educated woman, with a wonderful life, a loving family and many friends. I lived in a safe, healthy place. I was fully engaged and present in life. Or was I? No life is without stresses. How did I cope with my mine? I ran, hiked, biked, talked to friends, danced, played and had creative outlets like writing and painting. I sought out colleagues to discuss the stresses of work. I had many healthy coping strategies. What else did I do?

I ate.

I used food to cope with my anxieties, my fears, and my pain—just like any other addict. This realization was huge. I recognized a hidden part of me, one that wanted to be seen and heard. I finally understood that my relationship with food was destructive. I was a slave, I felt powerless and often out of control. Going on another diet was not going to fix this. I needed to go deeper, to uncover why I was using food to manage my emotions and, ultimately, I needed to change my relationship with food. I wrote a letter to my lover:

Dear Food,

Thank you for being there for me for so much of my life. You have been my solace in my times of need, my comfort from my pain. You have been a willing partner, always ready to slide down my throat, soothe the fire inside with your creamy sweetness. You have been a wonderful distraction to quell the loneliness of being human, keeping me busy buying the many parts of you, reading about you, cooking you, then ultimately devouring you.

Yes, from time to time you haven't lived up to my expectations, but that was never your fault. After all, I have been so very needy. But you, in all your innocence have been there; ready to help me shove down my anxieties, my fears, ready to reward me when I am tired and unappreciated. You have been there to divert my procrastination disguised as boredom, my sometimes-paralytic immobility. And most of all, you have helped me with my sadness, my sorrow that I so often did not even recognize. I especially thank you for that.

Although I feel indebted to you for all you have done for me, I want you to know this relationship is about to change. I still want and need you in my life but I am determined to be more conscious of how, where and when that happens. I hope you understand. It's time to take back my power.

With love and appreciation,
Nancy

As I embarked on this new journey, I metaphorically left my lover, a relationship filled with wonderful experiences, but also filled with confusion and turmoil, shame and anxiety. I was moving on to a new relationship with myself, even though I was not totally sure what that looked like. I'm still learning.

This journey has brought wonderful experiences, frightening experiences and sad ones. To venture into the hidden corners of self takes courage and resolve. It is so much easier to ignore, to turn away from self and stuff down. But in those corners lie the hungry child, the one looking for attention and love, longing to be fed. I have learned to hear my inner voice by turning with intent toward the needy parts inside me, learning to pause before reaching for food and give myself what it is I truly hunger for in a more loving and respectful way.

While creating this work, a number of brave people contributed their stories. Their names and circumstances have been changed but the narratives are their own.

"There's a franticness, a harried feeling, a scatteredness to addiction—I'm there but not there—I may appear there—I'm a good actor or maybe just skilled at doing multiple things at once—but my mind—it's buzzing—a piece, tiny or sometimes a big chunk is thinking about food and weight—obsessing, searching for something, something to swallow."

From the journal of NR

CHAPTER ONE

———

Addiction: The Invisible Pull

OVEREATERS ARE ADDICTS—FOOD is simply the drug of choice. I wrestled with using the term 'food addict' versus the more benign term 'overeater', but decided not to sugarcoat it. In order to change behavior, the first step is to face facts fully and honestly. The evidence of addiction speaks for itself. We go on diets, employ personal trainers and lose forty pounds. We eat foods that fuel our bodies and give us optimum energy per calorie, and we exercise to take off the excess weight. So why can't the weight loss be maintained? Why is it that over 90 percent of all people who embark upon a diet program do not find success?[1] The excuses can include:

➢ Healthy food is too expensive.

➢ It takes too much time to cook healthily.

➢ Who has time for exercise?

➢ I hate exercise.

➢ I come from a family of fatties; my weight is genetic.

➢ My family eats fatty foods, how do you expect me not to?

➢ I'm hungry all the time. I have to eat a lot.

The explanations are as diverse as the dieters.

What really happens is daily life. Our busy-ness gets in the way; the stresses sneak in and multiply. Old wounds fester, and new hurts are inflicted. The food addict turns to the place they are certain to find comfort: food. The degree to which addictive eating interferes with a person's life is on a continuum, from minimal to extreme. And, at some level, addictive behavior fits into the realm of the normal human experience. We have all engaged in addictive behavior on occasion, and employed unhealthy coping strategies to manage what we perceive as negative feelings or situations. Examples include excessive time spent watching TV or surfing the Net, escapes into one novel after another, chronic shopping, harmful and excessive sexual behavior, and alcohol and/or other substance abuse. The list of what human beings do to avoid negative emotions and situations is varied and seemingly endless.

How do we know when our behavior is a temporary way to avoid or cope, or when it has become a true addiction? I like Gabor Mate's clear explanation in his book on addiction, *In the Realm of Hungry Ghosts*:

"Addiction is any repeated behavior, substance-related or not, in which a person feels compelled to persist, regardless of its negative impact on his life and the lives of others."[2]

That's me! That's what I do! Busy with the kitchen mess after eating a great meal shared with friends and family, I find myself 'cleaning' up the edges of the pie. It's not because I'm remotely hungry. Yet that pie calls to me, like a siren's song, like how I imagine a pile of cocaine would call to a coke addict. It pulls me in with its seductive red berries and before I know it, the generous leftover, enough for two, has been whittled down to a scrawny portion for one. I will finish off that morsel later, bent over, head in the fridge, just before bed. I tell myself no one will notice, and ignore the fact that my ever-expanding bottom is a dead give away.

No matter how much the scales go up, the doctor threatens, and the clothes don't fit, food addicts do not stop overeating. The behavior is compulsive; relapse is regular, despite heartfelt promises to start afresh on Monday morning. No matter how determined, we find ourselves overeating again. We hate ourselves for it, which makes us irritable; we withdraw; we go into a spiral of dark, self-loathing thinking that ultimately compels us to eat, yet again. To see chronic overeating through the lens of addiction can set you free. It allows one to work with this issue in a different way, where it is possible to achieve success.

Julie is a tiny, round, professional woman in her late fifties with a sharp inquisitive mind and an endearing laugh. Having wrestled with weight issues most of her adult life, she realizes that understanding her overeating as an addiction, "... has actually helped me, it has made me less mean to myself. When I think of drug or alcohol addicts, I am always compassionate about their addiction. So, when I think of my struggles with food as an addiction rather than just a lack of willpower on my part, I am far more compassionate to myself. This kindness has had a profound effect on my psyche and my relationship with food." By naming the behavior as addiction, Julie was able to find empathy for herself.

All addictions—from addictions that are substance based, like alcohol and cigarettes, to addictions that are more about behavior, such as shopping and gambling—are attempts to change brain chemistry. We are driven to replace one feeling, usually negative, with another more positive feeling. In our society some addictions are actually respected and are seen as signs of achievement: A marathon runner could be addicted to the endorphin high that running provides, ignoring injuries, sometimes with long-term negative consequences. Yet this addiction creates elite athletes, winners. And exercise addiction has the added bonus of keeping us thin.

The workaholic who has climbed the corporate ladder, owns a boat, numerous cars, works of art, a summer home, is revered and deemed important despite never seeing his children. What about the slim food addict, the one who has the same obsession about food as the obese person, who regularly eats for emotional reasons but doesn't gain weight and jokes about having a tapeworm? No one ridicules her—she is envied. But food addicts who are fat are different. They are low on the totem pole of what is socially acceptable. Excluding the small population who sees weight as a badge of honor, (however, I suspect even this is a façade) the obese are still predominately viewed as disgusting, shunned by society, seen as weak and pathetic. Go on a diet and lose that weight for God's sake! How could you ever let yourself go like that? Glutton!

When we look closely at food addiction, it becomes obvious that food itself is not the crux of the problem. Although some foods have addictive properties, such as the caffeine in chocolate, few people are overweight from overeating chocolate alone. And although there is evidence that addiction to carbohydrates is a real phenomenon, again what is really at work is an addiction to the change in brain chemistry, in this case a hit of serotonin, the 'feel good' chemical.[3]

Some food addicts are addicted to the whole process, one that includes the planning, procurement and sometimes the preparation of the food, followed by the act of chewing and swallowing. We may think we are addicted to the pleasant taste sensations, but we are mainly addicted to the distraction from our feelings and the emotional numbing we experience when we stuff ourselves. The central problem, unlike most other addictive behaviors, is that we can't live without food. Hence, in order to beat food addiction, we cannot throw the proverbial 'baby out with the bathwater'. The goal is to learn to enjoy food as one of our earthly pleasures, yet end the addiction.

There is an obsessive quality with addiction, a focus that takes over and distracts us from everything else in our lives. Food addicts spend enormous amounts of time thinking-talking-reading about food, shopping for food and eating out. We love cooking shows, cookbooks and adore food photography. We are truly 'foodies'. Of course not every food addict fits this profile. And not all 'foodies' or people who are passionate about food are addicted. The difference is whether this self-proclaimed passion is in fact an obsession. An obsession is a colossal diversion, a place to fixate and spend a lot of time and energy, usually an unconscious way to avoid. And we justify the behavior:

> ➤ I love to cook.
> ➤ I have to feed the family.
> ➤ It would be insulting not to eat what someone has prepared for me.
> ➤ The food is going to go bad if I don't eat it. It's a sin to throw it out.
> ➤ I better eat that last piece of pizza, I have a long drive home.
> ➤ I have to taste everything, it's my responsibility, I'm the chef!
> ➤ Better eat another piece of toast or I will be starving by lunchtime.

It's a fine line between passion and addiction and it's a line that is not always clear.

However, sometimes it is crystal clear. In my worst binges I feel like a crazed woman. A part of my brain keeps scanning: 'What's to eat? What should I get next? Oh, maybe I'll go for the . . .' The obsession doesn't stop, I get pulled, find myself back in the kitchen, back in the fridge, scooping, tasting, shoveling. I feel detached from myself, watching through plate glass, removed and unable to stop.

The spiritual leader, Eckhart Tolle, explains addiction as:

"A long-standing compulsive behavior pattern may be called an addiction, and an addiction lives inside you as a quasi-entity or subpersonality, an energy field that periodically takes you over completely. It even takes over your mind, the voice in your head, which then becomes the voice of addiction."[4]

Addictions make us feel like a person possessed. This behavior is clearly not about a love of food, as anyone who has ever binged could attest to.

Julie reports, "I'm often not 'aware' in the moment. I become aware at the end the session. It's as if I have blinders on during the binge. I'm not thinking rationally and I think that's the point. I'm detached from the behavior. It is in control, not me." This quasi-entity or subpersonality can be so strong that the food addict feels helpless, like a marionette with someone else pulling the strings.

Conversely, food addicts are sometimes fully aware they are engaged in addictive behavior, yet continue to do so. Linda is a dynamic 43-year-old woman raising a blended family with her second husband. The youngest of six children, Linda grew up with a verbally and emotionally abusive alcoholic father and an enabling mother who coped by seeking the attention of other men. She had little time for her children. Linda became the invisible child, withdrawn and voiceless amidst the chaos.

When I asked what percentage of time she is conscious of her addictive behavior, she quickly answered 80 percent of the time. When asked why she continues the behavior, she responded, "It's like I'm trying to fill an unfillable void, it's like I'm overtaken by a need. I realized it filled the loneliness I felt as a child; food was always there even when no one else was. Then it became a way to silently get back at people: I'll show you, you can't tell me what to do. It was a way for me to strike out, yet really not hurt anyone else. Now it's no help at all."

When we first engage in addictive behavior, it is helpful. Our addiction of choice keeps the pain away long enough to attend schools, make friends, get jobs and be a part of the greater society. We choose our addictive behaviors instinctively, like grabbing a life ring, trying to survive the stormy seas of our childhood and/or events we don't know how to deal with. Addictions are a form of coping that start out serving the master, but in the end, the master becomes the slave.

Addictions keep us away from others and from ourselves. The more serious the addiction, the less we are truly home in our bodies. We're preoccupied, lost in our thoughts and obsessed with how to score the next hit. We are not engaged with others, we are not engaged with ourselves. Our attention is diverted from feelings and situations we find hard to live with. When we binge, the characteristic expression of addictive eating, we end up in an other-worldly state where everything else around us diminishes, fades into the background while we continue the binge. The binge is a classic representation of going AWOL from ourselves, numbing out with food, lost in a behavior where feelings and thoughts are suspended. It's the perfect diversion.

When I am lost in my own world, unaware and not fully present, my energy is often angry. I've been nibbling at the leftover cheesecake for two days, and am shocked and annoyed that I'm up a pound. Gone off in my obsessive insanity, I feel like somebody has done this to me. My husband calls and asks if I want to meet him for lunch and I make up some excuse. I am ashamed, not worthy, bent on starting another ridiculous diet, and miss out on an opportunity to connect with a person I love. And so it goes.

Addictions are interchangeable. Once we recognize overeating as an addiction, it is time to look at the other addictions employed in the quest to soothe our anxieties and fears, our sorrows and worries. Alcohol and drugs, excessive exercise—cleaning—working, and let's not forget the modern malady, shopping, are some of the ways we attempt to escape. Your colleague blames his thirty-pound weight gain on rediscovering his taste buds after quitting smoking. Not likely: the real truth is he has found another way to manage his feelings. If we continue to ignore and avoid what it is we are hungry for, we will exchange one addiction for another and engage in multiple behaviors that keep us stuck, spinning and wondering why things aren't working for us.

Because food is a literal representation of nourishment, it makes sense that what the food addict is hungry for is some comfort. When wandering around the kitchen looking for something to eat in that trance state—not physiologically hungry but hungry for something unidentified—we don't reach for a plate of carrot sticks. We go for comfort food, something warm, smooth, soft and sweet, or something crunchy, salty, fatty. Our need is to feel satisfied, satiated and full. Our need is to feel consoled, calmed and connected—loved on a basic visceral level, like being at our mothers' breasts. We don't know how to meet this need consciously, so eating works—to a point. Of course this is only temporary, we get distracted from what we feel, numbed out by food until the cycle starts again.

Food addictions range from fairly benign behavior to life threatening. Some food addicts are in complete denial because they do not carry extra weight for numerous reasons including exercise addiction. Three hours of exercise a day will keep the weight off for most of us. I didn't see myself as a food addict for years, partly because I fell into the more benign range. So what if I carry a few extra pounds? So what if I regularly stuff myself? I'm tall, active, and I don't have any health issues; I can pull it off. But as I approached my fifties and the few extra pounds turned into twenty, that little voice in my head told me that carrying extra weight was not good for my health. And I could no longer pretend that I was not using food to cope.

What really disturbed me is I felt like a fraud. I knew that if I couldn't deal with my addiction to food, I couldn't genuinely and authentically work with people who had serious, debilitating addictions, people who were caught in the terrible cycle of addiction, with seemingly no way out. I owed it to my clients to go deeper into my own story, uncover what was driving me and find ways to stop the behavior so I could offer them real hope from an authentic voice.

We need to identify our stresses, face our fears and the demons that send us to the fridge. Admitting our addiction is the first step in recovery. By telling the truth we step away from the dark trap of shame and denial, and step into the light where change is possible.

"What is the point, things will never change, I will never get a handle on this thing, I may as well face it, I will be battling this for the rest of my life."

From the journal of NR

CHAPTER TWO

———

Recognizing Patterns: The Yarns We Spin

WE MAKE NUMEROUS decisions daily. We make important decisions such as where to live, whether and whom to marry, how to earn a living and we make less important such as decisions such as, should I buy a new socket wrench or keep working with the old beat up one I already have. Decisions, decisions, decisions, all day, every day. Making an important decision, like deciding to change our relationship with food—to end the addiction—has the potential to alter our lives. Yet sticking with this choice in the days, weeks and months ahead is easier said than done, in part because of the unexamined dialogues that run through our heads; the stories that keep our belief systems intact, the stories that create our unique truths about life. Until we take the time to do the introspective work and uncover our belief systems, important parts of our stories will remain in the dark, layered in dust like forgotten letters from so long ago.

Losing weight and keeping it off has little to do with the popular notion of willpower or the suggestion that sheer will and determination will get results. The perception is that if one charges straight-ahead, jaw set, eyes fixed, the goal will be reached. This kind of resolve may be true in some situations, like getting through housework, but has not proven effective with addictive behaviors. To stick with the decision to lose weight and keep it off permanently actually involves the opposite behavior, a softening, a slowing down and becoming quiet within ourselves. When we are quiet, we clear a space to expose the specific pieces of the story that sabotage our weight loss plans. Stories handed down to us from our families, schools, churches and cultures—directly or indirectly—weave an interesting, albeit useless, yarn about what is or is not possible. These stories damage our chances for success and we don't even realize it. Thus, another piece of the puzzle in creating a healthy relationship with food is knowing our own stories.

One effective tool we can use to enhance the process of learning from our stories is journaling. When embarking upon a healing journey, recording your thoughts without censorship can deepen the experience and provide clarity. Writing helps illuminate thoughts, which can lead to new insights. I recommend treating yourself to a finely made notebook; use it like a friend. Or for the more techie types, create a place on your computer, a special file to lay down your thoughts. Whatever works. Some people believe journaling is about spilling their guts, writing down a lot of negativity. Although it may seem like that, it is more about revealing in a tangible way one's own fears and truths. It takes our thoughts that swirl away inside of our head and put them down in front of us where they have the potential to be dissected, rewritten and worked with. (Journal writing tips can be found on page 117).

Our monologue, commonly called self-talk, is our truth. When we write down our truth, we give ourselves the opportunity to really see our beliefs, our rules, sentence-by-sentence, and to expose as many as possible, no matter how strange or unimportant they seem. Be curious and open. Write freely whatever comes to mind; be wary of self-judgment, which impedes the process by stifling the flow of thoughts. The absence of self-censorship creates an opportunity to decide if we want to keep that belief or story, whittle it down, rewrite it or totally throw it out. The following is a list of possible stories that may impede our success:

- ➢ I can never lose weight.
- ➢ I will have to starve myself in order to keep my weight off.
- ➢ I will never be able to eat the things I like.
- ➢ I have slow metabolism.
- ➢ I love to cook and I love to eat; I am not giving that up.
- ➢ I am too lazy to exercise.
- ➢ My weight is genetic; it is beyond my control.
- ➢ I have no willpower.
- ➢ I am too weak.
- ➢ Most of my family is fat by the time they reach middle age.

Familiar? The last one is a particularly common story, one that is easy to back up with evidence. Look at your ancestors; the truth is there for all to see. But when we expose our beliefs we may find out there are other versions to the story. Could it be that large, rich meals are one way your family connects, celebrates life and each other? Is it possible that you come from a culture where eating big helpings of food is a sign of appreciation to the cook? Maybe your grandparents were incarcerated during times of war, and the legacy they passed down was a belief that being fat equated to peace, health and prosperity. Possibly food is the one great comfort that shielded them from their fears of poverty.

When we sift through our belief closet and take out those old outfits, our favorites that we used to look so good in, and try them on, do they still fit? Do they still express who we are? Or do they look ridiculous on us? Are we holding onto beliefs that have long ago outlived their usefulness, just because they have always been there and we haven't gone to the back of the closet and taken a look?

Examine your beliefs. Again, use your journal. Do they hold up under scrutiny? There are so many variations of the stories we tell ourselves when we ponder our inability to lose weight. Listen to the voice, notice if it tells a negative, dead end story about your battle with food addiction. Is there any room for change in that story?

On my journey to end food addiction, I became aware of a belief I held that greatly harmed my chances of success. I believed that I would eventually be able to manage my addiction to food but would probably never truly beat it. I believed that the pull to overeat would always be there and I would just get really good at handling it. This belief was so ingrained and yet I didn't noticed it. It was not until I met a woman who talked about her eating addiction in the past tense, sharing that the pull to overeat had completely vanished for her that I heard for the first time the story I told myself. Once that belief was exposed, I mulled it over for some time until I could open up to the possibility of a new story. I decided my new belief would be that "I enjoy a wonderful, loving relationship with food." I'm making that a reality.

When we listen and truly hear our voice, we will notice that our negative stories have two main actors: the victim and the judge.

The victim says:

➤ I can't help it; people don't realize the stress I'm under.
➤ I don't have time to shop, cook and eat well.
➤ I certainly don't have time to exercise.
➤ No one appreciates how hard I work.
➤ I have to do everything myself around here!
➤ I may as well have another cookie, what does it matter?
➤ I deserve some happiness.

The judge says:

➤ You're such a loser.
➤ You will never beat this thing,
➤ You have tried a million times, give up and accept the facts.
➤ This time won't be any different; you have no willpower.
➤ Face it—you will always be fat.

For some, one voice is louder than the other, but most of us vacillate unaware between the two. Because we so often can't hear our script, these negative voices become an undetected yet integral part of ourselves.

The victim's story may have become comfortable. Linda remembers: "I think I would tell myself, you are not worth it and you're nobody to anybody . . . nobody is going to listen, nobody will ever understand." This story was so ingrained that it was no surprise that Linda's first husband was emotionally and verbally abusive like her father. To Linda, this abuse was normal. Our defeatist's stories console us, give us permission to stay stuck, and reinforces the pointlessness of trying to change. They also give us permission to eat.

The judge speaks with a level of cruelty that is shocking. Most of us would never speak to others with the kind of disrespect and meanness that we feel is a perfectly acceptable way to speak to ourselves. Julie's increased awareness helped her hear her judge voice. "I regularly called myself a fat cow, told myself I looked disgusting in those jeans, that top, whatever. Revolting and disgusting were words I thought nothing of using to describe myself to myself." To see oneself as a fat cow, disgusting and revolting is tragic. But this dead end, body-loathing language is far too common. Who among us has not said or thought something similar? Yet we barely notice the unforgiving, hurtful ways we speak to ourselves and when we do, we justify it.

There are many who believe that what we say to ourselves becomes our reality. In other words, we manifest it. This is supported by the theories of the law of attraction. The idea that there is a basic universal law that says that what we think about, and what we say in our head or out loud is what we attract into our lives. Many believe this law is as real as the law of gravity. If I really believe that losing weight and keeping it off for good isn't possible, that belief will become my truth. The law of attraction states that this belief sends out negative vibrations and to allow, or make room for change, there must be an absence of negative vibrations. This theory validates how important it is to expose our negative self-talk when we attempt to change patterns of behavior.

How do we change our inner script, a story that is a fundamental part of us, a story we know so well and defend with vigor? First we have to see it. Human beings are blessed with an ability to do something that no other species can: the ability to observe our own thinking. A part of our brain called the prefrontal cortex, a relatively new area on the evolutionary scale, has the unique capability to read its own script, note the feelings, and make a choice before engaging in a behavior. This relatively small area of the brain is the head honcho, our own personal witness.[5] One of its jobs is managing our brain stem or the reptilian brain that is much more primitive. The reptilian brain, ingrained and ancient, controls our basic survival functions including alerting us to danger. So the prefrontal cortex has a big job to do. It puts the brakes on our behavior, including addictive behavior that the reptilian section is pushing for. It's like David taming Goliath. Goliath, like the addict, is trying to survive by turning to the substance or behavior of choice when emotions are too much. And David is just trying to help Goliath make better decisions.

It is essential to note that, for a small percentage of the population, the capacity to see one's own thoughts, combined with the ability to rewrite them and make different choices, is extremely difficult. The brain wiring required for this process may have been compromised in the uterus and/or by early childhood experiences. The majority of severely addicted people have experienced considerable early childhood abuse and neglect. These experiences can interfere with emotional freedom, or some call it emotional intelligence, which is the ability to see, understand and respond appropriately to one's own emotions and the emotions of others.[6] A child that is feels safe and loved has a chance to develop emotional freedom because they are not spending their energy trying to survive. Being able to break free from automatic responses that govern survival is much more difficult for those folks but not necessarily impossible. Professional help is highly recommended.

When we slow down enough to read the lines of the stories we write and then attend to the emotions that come up, change is possible. In the moments between registering a thought and taking action, there is an opportunity to stop, breathe, write a different story and choose a different action. Being able to understand and become intimate with the saboteur's voice in your head is imperative before going forward. To listen and expose the negative story with compassion and caring helps quiet the voice. Think of the negative voice as a scared child, one who needs to be picked up, rocked and embraced. When a child cries or whines and needs attention we can see that turning toward that behavior reduces his or her fear. When we ignore or scold the child, the child actually gets louder and more fretful.

Some call the saboteur's voice the 'shadow side' or the 'dark side', the thoughts we turn away from, ignore, stuff with food and other behavior. To embrace this aspect of self, to allow that voice to be heard, and to become honest with yourself safeguards you from the addict's best friend: denial. Conscious or unconscious, denial is a tactic we employ to pretend there is no problem. Addicts turn away from their own thoughts and behaviors and create elaborate narratives in an attempt to minimize and defend their choices.

My years of endless diets are a classic example of how I denied my addiction. "If I eat perfectly and exercise vigorously, I will be thin." I would set out with conviction on yet another diet plan, enjoy a little success, some weight would come off, I'd feel in control and often a little smug. I would then start sneaking handfuls of this and spoonfuls of that, tastes of anything and everything. Who exactly did I think I was fooling? My mind would say (if it registered the behavior at all) that this wasn't a big deal; these little bites would not hurt me. But of course that wasn't true and the pounds would creep back on, the pants would get tight again and I would be back to my pre-diet weight plus some, dumbfounded to find myself there. That is the astounding power of denial.

Then the shame sneaks in. "I blew it again." Mortified with my latest failure, the shame talk threw me back into the negative loop, feeling badly about myself, telling a story of how weak and pathetic I was—a story I silenced with food. Inside the cycle of addiction there is always the cycle of shame.

Julie realized that shame played a starring role in the cast of characters in her head. "I felt enormous pressure to be good. I was terrified of being shamed or embarrassed by others' comments or by my own actions. I became a pleaser who lived in terror that if people knew the real me they would be horrified." Julie is now learning to see her pleaser self in action and make different choices, better choices for herself that are not based in the fear of being rejected.

In the up part of the cycle we make so many promises:

> I'm not going to overeat.
> I'll stay away from the dessert table.
> I've been good for a week and I am not going to blow it.
> If I run for an hour I can have that butter tart.
> I won't have much dinner so I can eat this big lunch.

It doesn't happen; the saboteur or the devil on your shoulder whispers: "You deserve it, you worked so hard; it will taste so good, that creamy sweet goodness; tomorrow is another day."

You take a piece of pie, gobble it quick, then go back for the cake, popping a chocolate in your mouth while finishing off your daughter's cookie. Later, while you change for bed, you catch a glimpse of yourself in the mirror, notice the roll, the twelve extra pounds around your middle, avert your eyes, feel the shame, and start the punishing self-talk again. You vow to be different tomorrow.

Julie's being good story is a version of the 'I have to be perfect' belief. Most people would agree that nobody is perfect; yet they are terribly hard on themselves when they make what they perceive to be a mistake. When you dig deeper into your beliefs, you may find you really do hold onto an ideal of perfection. You may feel ashamed that you don't wear the same size jeans that you wore five years ago. We often have unrealistic expectations of ourselves in many areas of our lives, not just weight loss. If you have the 'I must be perfect' belief, you will inevitably fall short of your expectations and that disappointment may lead you to overeat.

Julie learned very young that not being perfect, making mistakes was dangerous and could result in adults withholding their love and approval. Julie spent her life in the tragic pursuit of perfection; if she got it right, she felt safe. She finally realized that, "When I stopped worrying about what other people thought and started thinking, 'What do I think'? I started liking myself more and therefore became happier." She learned to hear, then quiet that critical voice and replace it with one that was kinder.

There is a cast of supporting actors, along with the victim and the judge, who share the stage in our minds. Some parts of self are like armor, used to protect us against perceived threats. We have rehearsed these parts, and perfected the scripts for these characters that make up our personalities. One of my parts that I am not particularly proud of is 'the righteous girl'. She was developed long ago as a way to cope, a way to be in the know when she didn't know, or felt scared and confused. I perfected this role, found articulate language to back her; she has served me well and still pops up for bit parts, hopefully not as many full performances. She was one of the unrecognized shields I used to stay safe.

These aspects of self are rarely planned. They are the pieces we blindly grab on to because they fit our temperament, and are created from the circumstances of our childhood and our ongoing experiences. These characters keep us afloat, keep us from drowning in the soup of we are thrown into. If you are quick to anger, the mice scatter, people don't come close. It works. Anger, humor, arrogance, sarcasm, intellect and helplessness are just some of the many weapons we use to control. These behaviors, so called traits, are developed to protect us from feeling vulnerable, push underground the frightening thoughts and feelings most of us are not aware we have.

Mike is a barrel-chested 39-year-old writer/stay-at-home dad who takes care of his three children, two school aged and one four year old still at home. During our session, he stares pensively out his window and watches the neighbor's cat stalking a bird; I sit waiting for his response to my question regarding how looking at his past has helped him with his food addiction. He finally replies in his lovely Irish lilt, still audible after twenty years in Canada:

"There would have been no way to address my relationship with food without uncovering the deep beliefs and fears that were driving my eating behavior. I'm eating mindlessly for a reason. I am not fond of thinking about those reasons. But what it boiled down to for me was recognizing that the first step in changing the behavior was to do the therapy. I had to look at how my family affected me. I knew if I could deal with those things directly, there would be nothing left that was dark and frightening for food to compensate for. It wasn't even necessary to draw a direct connection between a specific childhood event and food. Just airing and sweeping out the closet removed the phantom driver of my eating behavior."

Uncovering events from our past is not about trashing our parents and finding fault. I deeply believe that most parents do the best they can with the knowledge they have. I have raised two children of my own and I know they will have struggles directly related to the blind spots of my and my husband's parenting. It's unavoidable.

Like so many families, one message I received in my family of origin was that food is either good or bad. Bad food was considered a treat and treats were given out sparingly. My parents were attempting to provide healthy balanced diets; they did not have the money for extra snacks, so rare treats such as cookies became forbidden. And for humans, what is forbidden becomes what is desired. As a child I perfected the art of sneaking into the kitchen, taking the lid off the cookie jar, and escaping to my room undetected with my pilfered goods. I could open the clunky handle of our sixties model fridge soundlessly, shove some hidden tid-bit into my mouth and do a Houdini. So treats became illicit for me, a guilty pleasure that fed my addiction.

Another significant factor when exposing our inner story is to ponder the actual length of time we spend on our weight struggles. Women spend an incredible amount of time thinking, talking and reading (pardon the irony) about weight and all matters of subjects related. Women spend countless hours in conversations about what is the right thing to eat; the right exercise; the best new diet; when to eat; what is the right weight ratio; what is wrong with all our body parts; how bad we feel about the latest binge; how we will try to do better tomorrow. Misguided, we believe that obsessing about it will somehow help to make us thinner. It doesn't.

Intellectualizing and obsessing about the problem, staying in our heads feels safe. Staying in our heads keeps us out of our bodies where emotions live. We don't stay present with what is happening all around us, we withdraw into our world of obsessing and bingeing. We retreat from the present moment where life is being played out and remain a prisoner, locked in our addiction. It's a terrible truth when we consider all the time spent on this obsession that actually fuels the fire that keeps the weight on.

Finding the why behind food addiction is so important in the journey to change the relationship with food and stop the obsession. We need to uncover the rules, written or unwritten, and the stories that we are told and the stories we spin ourselves regarding who we are or who we are supposed to be. Discovering what we use to keep our fears away, and what actors or saboteurs show up, are revealed as we peel back the layers of our onions. And peeling onions may make us cry.

As human beings, we have a need to make sense of the events of our lives. Our discoveries help soothe the stress that comes with not knowing and give us our "ah ha" moments. These are moments where change is possible. Exposing that inner voice takes time and patience and can be a very difficult journey. Be gentle with yourself. Rewrite those messages in a loving way, and talk to yourself with the same patience and kindness you would extend to your best friend.

Your negative voice was not originally yours; the stories have been handed to you from numerous sources including societal expectations. Hand them back. As cliché as it may sound, we need to learn to speak to ourselves in a loving way today—regardless of the number on the scale.

In mathematical terms, when we change directions slightly and follow the trajectory, we end up in a remarkably different place. As with all addictions, it's imperative to expose our stories and beliefs, write them down and use that journal to understand and link their effects to our present day behavior, then go gently forward.

Questions and Contemplations to Explore in Your Journal:

1. Write an inventory of your weight loss and gain history.
2. Write down as many beliefs you hold about life, weight and food. For example: "I believe that no one would be interested in me unless I am thin." Or, "I believe that no one would want to have sex with me unless I am thin."
3. What are your current beliefs regarding your ability to succeed at weight loss?
4. What are your rules around food and eating?
5. Have you identified the judge voice in your head and what does the voice say?
6. Have you identified the victim voice in your head and what does the voice say?
7. Is there another voice?
8. What happens when you make a mistake? What do you say to yourself?
9. How do you protect yourself? What does your armor look like?
10. What weapons do you use?
11. In a 24-hour period, how much time do you spend thinking and talking about food?

CHAPTER THREE

———

Uncovering Emotions: Hunger By Any Other Name

IT IS OFTEN difficult to distinguish between what we think and what we feel, even harder to link these to how we behave. Being able to see our thoughts and notice what we feel in a visceral way is the key to understanding why we act as we do. Awareness of our thoughts and emotions increases the likelihood that we will make conscious, thoughtful choices instead of reacting in a knee-jerk way that does not serve us. Although this chapter focuses on the emotional component of food addiction, it is almost impossible to compartmentalize thoughts, feelings, and actions because these three critical factors do not work independently of each other. Still, the emotional aspect deserves extra consideration, as it is often a hidden part of the self that needs attention if we are to understand fully what it is that drives the food addict.

An obsession with food is a great distracter from the feelings that occur in the body. My friend Darlene recalls, "I was standing at the counter, listening to Lucy [her adult daughter] give me more reasons for her drinking, her lack of work, the general stuck place in her life, making up all kinds of ridiculous excuses that I have heard over and over. I found myself slicing off chunks of the banana bread I had just pulled from the oven and shoving piece after piece into my mouth. I suddenly saw myself, it was like I was in a movie and although the whole scene was pathetic, I just had to chuckle. I was shoving my disappointment and frustration right down my gullet."

In a moment of clarity, Darlene noticed what she was doing. Often, food addicts don't. We are unaware of the shift or change in our physiology that precedes the drive to eat. This change may range from a subtle, almost imperceptible change to an overwhelming flood of negative emotion. Linda explains her process: "I don't think I completely knew before or after what was going on internally. But, I would notice that something was not right within me; I would sense an uncomfortable feeling . . . even though I would not be able to name it. Naming feelings was not something I grew up with. Most of the time I was told what I was supposed to feel. So I learned to stifle my true emotions." For Linda and Darlene, when uncomfortable or conflicting feelings arise, food is the balm that soothes.

Food addicts often fear their feelings, especially feelings of hunger. We obsess about food, thinking of lunch as we eat breakfast. While enjoying lunch we plan dinner. As with many forms of fear, the fear of hunger is managed by control: Don't get hungry. Traveling snacks are packed; specific eating or snack restocking stops are mapped out in advance. Must not be without food. Consequently, many food addicts rarely feel true physiological hunger because we keep ourselves fed. What would happen if our stomach started to growl? What if we felt real hunger pangs?

I often joke that I must have starved in a previous life. For those who have felt the pain of true starvation, forgive my glibness. That pain is primal, real and terrifying. But I'm going to assume that, since you are reading this book, any experience of feeling extreme hunger has been self-inflicted, caused by dieting. The reality for most food addicts is that food is just a step away; the fridge is full and the cupboards are overflowing. So why do feelings of hunger strike such a chord of fear?

Studies show that humans register countless feelings in their gut. Many of our negative feelings, from mild to extreme, can be felt in the pit of the stomach. Think of the common ways people describe these feelings.

➢ I felt my stomach drop.
➢ I felt like I just got kicked in the guts.
➢ I felt my stomach flip over.
➢ Talk about having your guts ripped out.
➢ I had a gut feeling.
➢ I had butterflies in my stomach.
➢ It was gut wrenching.

Not always able to track the source of the negative gut feelings and fear rising, food addicts get confused. They believe that they are hungry and eat. And along with all the variations and combinations of gut feelings, buried inside us is one of the scariest feelings of all—emptiness.

Gabor Mate's son Daniel describes this emptiness beautifully in his father's book, *In the Realm of Hungry Ghosts*: "I, too, carry a void inside—nothing exotic, just an ordinary, human despair-fear-anxiety factory—and mine will try to feed on anything that gives me an instant sense of self-definition, purpose or worth."[1]

For some that place is not ordinary but extraordinary. This place is the beast within. A dark, frightening, intangible place that has been created from countless traumas, some that we are aware of, some not, and some we dare not ponder. Traumas are those events in our lives that are mini or major explosions, events we react to but may not fully understand how they impact the body. They are the experiences we are unable to process at the time or in the early aftermath, the incidents that get trapped in our bodies. Trauma may happen once, like a car crash, or be repetitive, like feeling humiliated and bullied regularly at school. The after-effects show up uninvited, sneak into our thoughts, provoke uncomfortable feelings, which in turn dictate our behavior: we eat. Handling the food, chewing and swallowing distract us from the feelings we may not consciously register. But our body knows to reach for something to push down those uncomfortable sensations, with our drug of choice.

We go home after work or after school, go straight to the kitchen, prepare dinner, something for the pan, something else for the mouth. Handfuls of cheese devoured while we grate it for the pasta. Why is it that the after-work/school time is such a trigger time for many food addicts? The stresses from the day have accumulated; we are on automatic pilot and going from one role to the next without pause or reflection.

Dr. Christianna Northrup explains in her book, *The Wisdom of Menopause*, that by late afternoon the main hormones that allow us to fight stress begin to lose strength and leave us more vulnerable to our underlying emotions. "In particular, when serotonin, the 'feel good' neurotransmitter, is depleted, we are apt to eat anything in sight—particularly refined carbohydrates—to bring it back to normal."[2]

When it has been hours since lunch, we're not as chemically resilient and our hunger makes us anxious. The feeling—similar to fear in the pit of the belly—isn't tolerated well. Lost in our thoughts, lost in our worries, lost in our fears, we don't feel the churn. We're on automatic pilot, not in the moment, ruminating about something that has happened or something that may happen; that's where anxiety lives—in the past and in the future. The beast within looks for relief.

That fear in the belly is not obvious to many of us because, along with stuffing ourselves, as addicts we employ effective strategies to mask our feelings. Anecdotally, I have noticed that among many talents, food addicts often overdo. We take care of things, work diligently and can be people others count on, unaware that the underlying motivation is to control our environment, make sure nothing goes wrong. If we control things, we won't feel the fear. Studies of adult children of alcoholics, who grew up in homes that were typically chaotic, show they tend to have high control needs. This need comes from an learned fear that if you are not in control, if something happens that you did not anticipate, chances are it is going to be bad, it is not going to turn out alright. Therefore the only solution is to plan to control your environment. Becoming super capable is not always the case, but it is a common reaction to growing up in dysfunction, and on the surface it looks good.

The fear in the belly has numerous sources but none as significant as what we experienced as children. Our experiences in the uterus, infancy and early childhood have a tremendous impact on our lives because it's a period of unparalleled brain development. Especially early in life, the brain is like a sponge soaking up its surroundings at an unprecedented rate. Infants are constantly taking the temperature of the energy in the room, instinctively looking for security and safety. Because babies and children have not yet developed the ability to make sense of their experiences, these experiences get buried at a deep, cellular level.

The following is another piece of my story.

Something is wrong, I can tell but I don't understand what it is. Everyone is mad. Dad, head down, eating, Mum with her eyebrows knit, a slight scowl. My older brother, shoveling his food, shoulders tense, eager to get out of here. My younger sister doesn't know enough to stay silent; she stirs things up, challenges and asks questions. There I am, at my place between my sister and my dad, eating but not tasting, getting through this meal, a typical dinner at our house, swallowing while observing, hypervigilant. Am I the only one who notices something is wrong?

Eat what is put in front of you. You're a kid; there is no deciding if you like the food or how much you're to eat. Just eat it. Dinner with my family was not fun; it was a job to get done. When I think back on this time (I believe I was about eight), what I remember primarily is feeling bewildered. I didn't understand. I didn't know why everybody was mad; it made no sense. I must have been scared. Any moment an argument could break out between my parents, my brother might stalk off, my sister might get slapped, my father would shout, "that's enough" in his gruff tone, and my mother would snap back at him, or us, or not react at all. I sat there, the classic middle child, and wondered how to stop it, wondered how to fix it.

I have no explicit memories of what it was like at the age of two, with a baby sister and a three-year-old brother. But I can guess. As anyone who has been around babies and young children knows, things would have been stressful. A family of five means five competing sets of needs. Not easy.

My own process has helped me understand that undetected feelings of anxiety and fear were associated with overeating. My pattern was to eat quickly and mindlessly. Doing my own therapy helped me make sense of what I could not comprehend as a child. My parents had three children by their mid-twenties. My father was making his way in the world, had a good job in a local plant, but went from the excitement and freedom of college life in Toronto, to having four extra people dependent on him within five short years. My mother struggled with severe asthma, while managing three kids under the age of three with the added stress of no health insurance. She was a creative, intelligent woman cast into the role of the fifties housewife, unable to question the fit. This time of their lives was no scene from a Hallmark card; it was hard work and they were doing the best they could. My father was raised by a practical, strict mother; my mother came from a family with eleven children. Dinner was about getting the family fed as efficiently as possible with minimal waste.

The adult part of me understands and knows that my parents did their best. I appreciate that the suffering of my childhood was minimal on a trauma scale. Many children endure far worse situations than I did. But the legacy of that experience was buried deep within me and needed to be unearthed so I could manage the effects instead of letting them manage me.

The impacts of our experiences play out in front of our eyes behaviorally when we react from that place. When we boast, engage in malicious gossip, continue to say yes to things we would prefer to say no to, shove food in our mouths when we aren't hungry, we are reacting to our underlying feelings. And let's not forget about our reactions based on the feeling of anger. How many times have we reacted in anger, justified it or became embarrassed, while not really understanding why we acted the way we did?

Anger is a powerful emotion, yet it is secondary. There is always another feeling underneath motivating it. Road rage is a display of extreme anger but the feeling that got triggered was fear. I thought he was going to hit me! Anger is confusing. Suppressing it makes us sick, yet raging out sends our blood pressure through the roof, which in the end makes us sick too. We don't know how to express it. The rules of how to express anger appropriately vary greatly between cultures, genders, and the norms of the times we live in. In our confusion we swing from extremes: become martyrs and suffer in silence, or anger overwhelms us and it boils over and leaves a mess. It is a complicated emotion worth further examination.

All the aspects of our journeys, including our families of origin and the society we move through, create the fear factories that operate within us. These include our negative experience in our various relationships, families, churches and schools, the impact of events in the greater society, accidents and illnesses. These are our traumas, from big-T traumas such as the death of a parent; to the accumulating effects of something less obvious that may be considered little-t traumas, such as being left alone each day after school before being emotionally ready. For the food addict, food is the substance that can quell these fears.

Mike recalls, "I definitely learned at some point to use food to comfort myself. It may be unfair, but my recollection of my mother is of her being too busy, distracted or attending to her own needs to be available to comfort and reassure me, except at mealtime. There's a part of me that believes I learned to equate eating with my mother's attention, even as a baby. Later, when I was a young boy, I remember receiving attention and praise when I would make something from a recipe. It would be a special time with my mother when we baked together. In any event, at age twelve, the time of my parent's divorce, I was allowed to use the kitchen by myself, and with all of the hurt around the house in connection with the divorce I began to cook a lot of food and eat it all." Mike's story is a telling example of how addictions form.

Our accumulated traumas live within us in the form of explicit and implicit memories. Explicit memories are those we visualize and have details for in a specific context, like the memories I have of sitting at the kitchen table eating dinner with my family. Implicit memories are the ones we can't see clearly, but which evoke emotion such as my unrecognized feelings of stress when sitting down to eat dinner.

What we remember and what we feel are not congruent. For me, I never could figure out why I ate so fast, literally inhaling my food as though there was a fire. When I took the time to remember and journal about my childhood dinners, I uncovered some memories that helped explain my actions. My experiences created an imperceptible anxiety around food. Once I noticed the feelings, I started to employ strategies to manage them and change the behavior.

The events in our lives range from what looks minimal on the trauma scale to the truly horrific. Only we can know how something has affected us, regardless of the judgment of others. A classic Buddhist story that illustrates this is the one about being struck by two darts.[3] The first dart hits and we react, but it is the second dart that is significant. Metaphorically, some may take that dart, pull it out, rub their shoulder and carry on. Others may faint, get taken by ambulance to the hospital, fret over infection and talk about the injury for a year. Neither case is right or wrong; they simply illustrate our individual reactions to events. The Buddha's story shows we have power over the meaning we make regarding our traumas, maybe not at the time in the case of infants and children, but at some point, by doing introspective work.

For many, it's easy to minimize the significance of trauma. Because mine were little-t traumas, it took years to link how those negative experiences impacted me. The fifties was not an era that encouraged talking about feelings, especially for children. Talking about one's pain was complaining and seen as indulgence. "If you don't have anything nice to say, don't say anything at all," was a typical rule of many households.

Linda remembers, "When my dad would get drunk and chaos would erupt in the house, after the arguing was over, my mom would put me in the car and we would go and get something sweet (an ice cream sundae or a donut). We wouldn't talk about what had happened, we just calmed ourselves with food, and pretended nothing had happened." This was Linda's normal. As often happens, the meaning—the second dart, was taught to her: Linda was taught to swallow her fear. Linda didn't know she carried trauma and it took time for her to make the link between these childhood events and her food addiction.

At the other end of the spectrum, some of us get stuck in our traumas, reliving them over and over again until they become our identities. Angry and hurt, we justify stuffing ourselves, because we deserve our one pleasure. These are all coping mechanisms, ways to maintain a victim status or minimize and deny the hurt—an addict's best defense. If it can't touch me, it won't hurt me. But our strategies don't really help and the pounds pile on.

There are theorists who believe that the level or seriousness of our addiction directly relates to the level of intensity and type of trauma. "Except in rare cases of physical disease," Mate writes "the more obese a person is, the more emotionally starved they have been at some crucial period in their life."[4] And emotional starvation takes on many forms, from severe abuse—physical, emotional and sexual—to the silent child abuse, neglect.

Again, I think it's important to note the failures of parents are rarely intentional. There are innumerable circumstances that impede a parent's ability to be present for their children. For example, dealing with a sick child, grieving a death, war, illness, divorce, caring for other family members, job responsibilities, poverty, addiction and mental illness. Parents are typically juggling many balls and trying to meet many demands. Consequently, some may fall terribly short on giving their children what they require. The more parents are absent physically or emotionally, the more children have to create their own connections and find their own comforts; that can lead to disastrous results.

Victims of abuse may use their layers of fat as protection. Fat is the house they have built around themselves. Consciously or unconsciously, excess weight may be used to keep away sexual attention, or may be a way to create bulk to feel more powerful. Fat is the armor. Fat is the shield to get on with life, be productive and not be swallowed-up by one's own pain.

Twenty years ago, Julie passed out inebriated at a party and woke up to a friend having sex with her. "It was years before even I labeled that experience as rape," she says now. "For the longest time, I blamed myself. I was the one who got so loaded. The real shame and guilt came when I found out I was pregnant. I didn't tell anybody about it, not a soul. At the time I remember thinking that this sort of thing didn't happen to ugly women, but I never thought, I'll become fat and then men won't be interested. It was more like food was a natural place to turn; it became just another secret to hide. The following year, I gained 50 pounds. It was years before I connected the dots and realized that the weight had literally created this protective barrier around me. It never occurred to me that the two incidents were related. As I look back, I can see that I was using food and booze to try and protect myself. It was the beginning of a life spent alone. I think now that I couldn't trust myself, let alone anyone else. How could I possibly trust another person? I have never really trusted another romantic partner since."

Tragically, Julie's experience is not an uncommon story. Despite the numerous therapists and agencies designed to help victims (male and female) of abuse work through their experiences, too many stay in the shadows. Feelings of shame keep them from seeking help and send them underground. They attempt to erase the experience, and addictions provide a welcome relief.

Emotional pain is one of the worst pains imaginable. You can't rub it and you can't put a salve on it. If we are perceptive we can see it revealed in our behaviors, although many times we are blind. Yet pain is always at the core of our addictive behaviors. Addictions are about self-medicating in order not to feel the ache of our past traumas, our wounds and the pain of our present-day situations. Self-medicating is an attempt to extinguish feelings we find intolerable.

We build our walls to protect ourselves, figuratively and literally. We don't know how to manage emotions without using food. When we lose some weight, we feel vulnerable and it scares us so we pack the fat back on, plus some more as fast as possible, like the turtle retreating back into the safety of its shell. We're home, safe and sound.

If fat as armor resonates, losing the extra weight and keeping it off for good can be akin to standing naked on the edge of a cliff, arms spread wide in a windstorm. Emotions are front and center and raw. Without a plan to manage the strong feelings of vulnerability that are bound to arise, it is nearly impossible to keep the weight off. This is at the heart of the phenomena of why, when we get to our goal weight, very few of us stay there.

When we decide to no longer use food to cope with our emotions, we may experience a grieving process, not unlike ending an illicit love affair. You know it's time, you know the affair is destructive, and you feel guilty most of the time. The actual good parts of the affair are long gone; now, there's more pain than pleasure. There's that emptiness again, a feeling of loss. How can you tell anybody, they would think you're crazy? Your friends saw how the relationship was destroying you and they are happy it's over.

When you lose weight, you get noticed and receive compliments. People are genuinely delighted for you, and your doctor is thrilled. But you miss your old lover: food. You may miss the gorging, the hours spent engaging in the eating process, and you miss the way the pudding slid down your throat taking the pain with it. Geneen Roth reminds of a central truth in her work, *When Food Is Love*,

"The hardest part about compulsion is that when the behavior ends, the emptiness does not."[5] We have to find a way to live with that.

Learning to recognize, name and handle emotions is a tremendous challenge. Doing this work can crack open old wounds that you may have been unaware of or kept covered. You have been carrying extra weight for a good reason. Trust that if you are reading this book, you are ready to look into these dark corners of self. Again, using your journal as your friend and therapist is a wonderful way to understand your process and see your behaviors. I highly recommend that you find a trusted buddy to support you through this work. If you feel the need, give yourself permission to seek professional help.

Questions and Contemplations to Explore in Your Journal:

1. Are there events you can remember that may have contributed to your addiction to food?
2. Have you ever gained or lost weight after a significant event?
3. Is there anyone else in your family of origin who may be addicted to food or other substances or behaviors?
4. Can you tell the difference between emotional hunger and physiological hunger? How?
5. Does physiological hunger scare you or send you into a panic?

CHAPTER FOUR

Stress: Stop the World— I Want to Get Off!

OUR CHILDHOOD EXPERIENCES are the wellspring that forms our present day behavior, but they are by no means the only source. Experiences throughout our lives, the times we live in, the stress we are under, the stress we create, our traumas, losses, sorrows and joys all shape our reactions and interpretations. And a new phenomenon, one that significantly impacts our emotional, physical and spiritual health is the sheer speed of change humanity has witnessed in the last hundred years. Unprecedented technological developments coupled with the amount of information we are flooded with are two clear examples of the extraordinary changes. It is often overwhelming.

And the information we are inundated with is predominately negative. Bad news is in our face every moment; images play on the multiple televisions that many North Americans have on simultaneously in different rooms in the house, and in public places such as restaurants, gyms, hotel lobbies, bars, even in airports, train stations and banks. Along with the bad news stories are the warnings of how we are to safeguard ourselves and manage these hypothetical disasters that lurk around each corner. Jon Kabat-Zinn, in his book *Full Catastrophe Living*, labels the effects from this onslaught of information as "World Stress"[1] an apt name to describe this 21st century phenomena.

We don't recognize how the torrent of bad news and the insistent advice about how to protect ourselves impacts us on a physical level and creates stress. We become fearful, vicariously traumatized, with no way to escape the flood of negativity. Yet 'world stress' pushes us to the limit, giving us literally endless scenarios to worry about. And we believe our obsession to 'be in the know'; to become so called 'news junkies' is a sign of intelligence and savvy. Must stay informed. If we shut out the information we feel moronic. If we don't use the latest safety device we feel negligent.

Discovering how outside influences affect our individual stress levels produces a choice point. When we acknowledge the impact of those stresses, we can look closer and limit the amount of information we invite into our living room. I peruse a weekend newspaper, news magazine articles and listen to some local and national radio. I do not follow the latest disaster stories and I now recognize that it is not from a place of indifference as I feared, but from a place of self-preservation. I can feel the stress mount in my body, feel my heart sink with every story of a child murdered by the hands of someone who supposedly loved them. Headlines announcing that a family of five has perished in a car accident make me cry. The stress these events create in my body does not change the reality of the tragedies, but I carry them. My body has a tipping point, a place where it is full up. I strive to recognize that point before I get there.

It's important to define your tipping point and author what you need; grant yourself permission to measure the toll that the suffering of humanity takes on your body. Notice the fear inside and learn how to look after it. This does not mean you don't care. It does not mean you won't strive for change, show compassion and do your bit. It just means following the flight attendant's instructions: Put your oxygen mask on first, before putting it on others.

Expectations

Another significant source of stress worth examination stems from our expectations. What constitutes a good life has increased dramatically in post-war North America. Advertising became big business in the mid-twentieth century, and found the perfect path into our homes via television and our ever-increasing appetite for newspaper and magazines. We now live in a society where we must be cleaner, faster, smarter, better cooks, fantastic lovers, keep wonderful homes, have straight, white teeth, be skinny, be the standard of 'good looking'; in truth, we are supposed to be perfect.

These are the 'shoulds'. Who we think we should be, how we should act, what we should say and do. We miss the signs of stress because we are busy, driven to perform and accomplish. We miss the signs because we may even feel energized and engaged, proud of our multitasking and appear to be able to keep those dozen balls in the air. Taking the lead in a project at work/school may be invigorating, you have a clear vision, a leadership role excites you and you are good at it. You pull it off, people are impressed, praise is lavished upon you, you achieve that coveted 'A' grade. While all of this may be true, that does not change the fact that hormone and adrenaline levels, which are designed to help us in alarmed states and get us ready for action, are increased. This chemical bath is important, it alerts us to danger and is an innate system designed to keep us safe. It is not designed to go off indefinitely. What your system can handle is individual. How much is too much?

Recognizing how the load affects your system is a matter of pausing, even when the load is 'good stuff'. It's about setting boundaries with yourself and others, about admitting that maybe you can't do it all. Be okay with the reality that the guy beside you may seem to cope with more, gets much more accomplished during the day and does not get phased by it. In reality that is a judgment; we never know what is truly going on in anyone else's life. It is also the comparison game, the one that you can never win. So stop playing.

Even if you are animated and engaged, the best juggler in the world, we all have a breaking point. This is not about eliminating stress from your life. Feeling stress is a normal part of being human and when we push ourselves within our personal limits we are often successful. Pushing beyond our personal limits is where stress lurks. It is about knowing when it's too much, when we cross the line and are in danger of overloading our system. Unnoticed and unattended stress sneaks in and if you're a food addict, you will gobble it up and keep on going.

Our identity is formed by circumstances, grabbing, usually mindlessly, what fits our temperament, birth order, family dynamics and experiences. This creates our so-called personality. If helping mama with your baby brother when you were four made her less angry, made her notice you and say nice things, you may develop 'the good little boy' persona. But you're now thirty-five, juggling a ridiculous load, over functioning for your wife and children, friends and colleagues. You love it when people notice and praise you, yet you downplay it, pooh-pooh it, say 'it was nothing'. When they don't notice, you are secretly resentful and tell yourself that it does not matter, 'I don't need the recognition'.

You're stuck in a dance you don't recognize that keeps you angry, just like your mother. You have never been allowed a voice, and haven't learned as an adult that you can speak. You stay caught, don't feel entitled to say the most precious word 'no', and your 'have to' list keeps getting bigger.

If we say no to the friend who is always in crisis, don't drop everything to rescue him once again on our precious Saturday night, it doesn't mean that we are uncaring and heartless. It may feel that way but by creating boundaries, and saying that simple word, we start to loosen the ties that bind us into old patterns of behavior. Play around with this concept, shift it, move it over a little. If one end of the continuum is a rescuer and the other end is a person who does nothing for anyone, try moving the needle a few notches toward the middle. Say yes to yourself. This is how we take care of ourselves.

Guilt will be the next feeling that causes stress when you learn to say no. Guilt is a feeling that we rid ourselves of by 'fixing it' or by 'rescuing'. This feeling is reinforced with an internal monologue about how people need us: we owe them, they won't manage if we don't do this or that, how everything will all unravel if we don't ride in on our white horse. But of course we can't really fix anything, our methods have limited effectiveness and often blow up in our face. At the end of the day, we can't really change anybody except ourselves. But we don't know that yet. We react when it doesn't work out. We eat our frustration. We swallow our resentment.

Assuming the role of a rescuer, a perfectionist/pleaser, or a combination of both is an unsustainable way of being. Something has to give. Saying no creates guilt that robs your sense of peace and well-being. But those feelings can be attended to, shifted and managed. Learning to deal with your guilt instead of letting it run you brings a welcome relief and opens you up to new choices.

There are many stresses that come from events beyond our control, caring for a sick partner; the loss of a job through no fault of our own; the stress caused by a disaster, manmade or natural such as a house fire, hurricane or a flood; and of course one of the biggest stresses of all; the death of someone we love. In the aftermath of losing my cousin and good friend to a sudden heart attack, I found my appetite, along with my feelings were mostly shut down. But within a year, the ten pounds I had successfully shed and had kept off for a couple of years crept back on. Again, I fell back into my typical style of coping, I talked about the experience, processed it to a point, yet carried on with my busy life while keeping my deeper feelings stuffed.

The stressful circumstances of our past experiences, our present lives, the stress we let in, the stress we create by our impossible standards all reside in the cells of our body and send off chemicals that wear down the internal organs and create feelings we strive to change. Left unattended, stress can build to the point of becoming a full-blown anxiety disorder. The highest incidence of relapse for food addicts, like all addicts, happens in times of stress. Identifying the source and managing stress is another piece in the puzzle to become free from food addiction.

Questions and Contemplations to Explore in Your Journal:

1. Do you recognize when you are stressed out?
2. What are the symptoms?
3. During time of stress, if there were a movie camera on you, what would you see?
4. How do world events affect you?
5. Does the concept of being perfect or a 'pleaser' resonate to you?
6. If you are aware of your fears and or stresses, what steps have you taken in the past to manage it?
7. What steps do you take now?
8. What story do you tell yourself that keeps you stressed out?

CHAPTER FIVE

———

Food and Hunger: What the Hell am I Supposed to Eat!

WADING THROUGH THE myriad of weight loss information is daunting and overwhelming. Each nugget of information speaks of the merits of good food versus bad food—which foods offer the fountain of youth and which foods are going to kill you. Just when we get comfortable, settle in with the latest 'truth', someone else comes along armed with scientific data the average person cannot begin to understand and refutes all prior claims. So off we go back to the diet drawing board. There are currently over 25,000 diet books in print.[1] That's a lot of different theories and a lot of contradictions. No wonder trying to lose weight is so frustrating!

Yet we are desperate to believe; we are excited about the latest research that is going to finally help us lose the weight for good. Eating up the new information, we bravely try the next diet, pushing back the voice that says, oh no, here we go again. Like lemmings, we scurry to join the pack and jump off the cliff, ignoring our imminent demise, caught up in the excitement of the crowd, filled with renewed faith and vigor. Ready to start afresh on Monday. Or just after this vacation. Right after New Years. We chronic dieters are a true testament to the human spirit.

We have become a nation of freaked-out consumers. Half the time we just don't know what to eat. The labels list dozens of ingredients in foods that claim to have no fat, low fat, high fiber, low fiber, no cholesterol, and/or no sugar. And if there is sugar, it may be real or artificial. It seems we need to become a lay scientist. Still we give it our all, becoming pseudo nutritional experts. Ask a diet junkie how many calories are in a piece of bread or a chocolate chip cookie, and undoubtedly he or she will know the answer. Most of us could write a diet book, we are that well versed. Sit around with a bunch of chronic dieters and ask what is the right way to lose weight and watch how passionate they become. Dieters will rattle off so-called 'truths', have more facts at their fingertips, get more fired up about this topic than almost any other. The debate ensues, opinions fly, and everyone has a theory he or she is attached to. Invariably there are some sad voices from the disillusioned, the ones who have given up, are defeated and have moved to a place of simply accepting the extra weight. The topic is mind-boggling.

Popular media contributes to our confusion. Check out any woman's magazine; sandwiched between the latest diet crazes are recipes and beautiful photos of food. 'Good' is represented in a bright cheery kitchen, blueberries atop a bowl of steaming oatmeal beside a pious housewife, smiling and righteous, with apple cheeks and a plastered-on smile. Conversely, 'evil' is displayed with great seduction, a gorgeous full-page photo of a chocolate cake, icing glistening, back dropped with red satin and a rose seductively laid at its altar. The forbidden fruit, designed to excite.

We don't dare admit it. We eat our chocolate cake in secret, riddled with guilt. We do not allow ourselves to savor it; we get through it like a hurried tryst, often with minimal enjoyment, desperate to not get caught. We have learned that we do not deserve to enjoy the cake in the open; cake is bad food, the desire for it is another mark of weakness on the long list of things to be ashamed of.

Is there really anything wrong with a piece of cake once in a while? Of course there isn't. We need to look at food not in terms of good and bad, but in terms of fuel quality, in terms of low test or high test. This sounds like semantics but it is important to determine how efficient the gas you put in your tank is, without demonizing certain kinds. Polarizing food creates stress. The goal is to have a relationship with food that feels good to you mentally and physically instead of one that is adversarial. Realistically, both qualities of fuel will run the machine; both qualities will get us from point A to point B. Yet we know that vehicles fed a better grade of fuel tend to run more efficiently and last longer. It is the same with humans. That cake will keep our engine running, thank you very much. We may sputter mid-day, enjoy a few large belches, and need a little nap, but we will keep moving forward and it probably won't kill us. If we ate this way daily, it would be another story.

To lose excess weight without embarking on yet another diet, to strictly adhere to a 'no-diet' rule (that includes cleanses and fasts) is truly challenging. Cleanses and fasts are designed to detoxify our bodies and promote health, but honestly, for chronic dieters they are another 'lose weight quick' scheme. If you are reading this book, most of you have tried every plan there is to try. We have spent far too much of our life talking, reading, discussing and going on diets. To make a commitment to become aware, we have to stop the diet mentality, with all the rules that tell us what to eat, what combination, what time of day to stop eating, how many calories is in this and how much fat in that. To choose to stop dieting for good, yet trusting that we can learn to interrupt our addictive behaviors takes bravery and ironically, an increase in awareness of your patterns.

There is one basic rule of mathematics, to lose weight and keep it off—one that sounds like a diet—you have to burn more calories than you consume. Therefore, before you can change your relationship with food and become an intuitive eater (a person who hears and gives their body what it needs naturally) you must increase your awareness of how much you are ingesting today. This may feel even more obsessive for a time, getting to know the what, where and when, the details and patterns of your consumption. But to beat an addiction one needs to get real and clear. Food addicts, like all addicts, minimize and deny what they consume.

Personally, I resisted writing down what I ate. It reminded me of one too many diets. I tried to ignore and play down my sneaky, bingey ways. But the third helping of crusty bread, slathered in butter at dinner was hard to deny when it stared back at me from the pages of my journal. (You would think the roll on my gut would have been a dead giveaway)! So I succumbed and wrote down what I ate just to see my consumption laid out in front of me in black and white. (For some reason I felt less resistant when I tracked what I ate on my computer, so do whatever works). I needed to see the behavior, without denial, justifications and excuses. Again, this may feel contradictory and confusing, being first asked to examine an obsession before letting go of it but what is born out of our greatest confusion is clarity.

Becoming an intuitive eater means listening to your body's wisdom and being able to discern the difference between wants and needs. My body was always trying to tell me what it needed; I did not listen. I just fed it. My habitual after dinner snacks were cookies, chocolate, ice cream, or some such sweet, whether I was hungry or not. But I learned that these foods tend to affect my sleep, especially when I ate too much. I would start to fall asleep, be jolted awake with heart palpitations and a little adrenaline surge. As I age, I have noticed an increased sensitivity to sugar. So if I truly feel biological hunger, I try to pick foods that my system responds well to. My success rate soars when I am notice and manage my emotions.

When I learned to examine my routines, the what, where and when of my eating and how foods affect me, I was able to start addressing the negative patterns and was on my way to becoming an intuitive eater. The following are some suggestions to help you hear your inner voice, your body's needs, see your behaviors and generally increase awareness of your own process.

First Step—Becoming Conscious

Get out that journal and try to give yourself at least two weeks to become conscious of what you eat, how much (categorize simply into small, medium and large amounts, assuming you are honest about the difference), what time of day, where you were and what emotional state you were in. Be truthful, uncensored and brutally candid. The only rule is no judgment! This is not an exercise to beat yourself up. This is about pure honesty. Remember, we are addicts and we lie, to others and to ourselves.

Some folks think two weeks is too long, they want to get on with this, lose that weight. That is diet mentality and what we are trying to do is end addictive patterns. So get curious. If you want to formalize this process, pick a time each day. Think about what was going on for you, what preceded your overeating from a mild to full binge. You want to start to track your binge triggers. Remember, if you have decided to change your relationship with food you need to understand the intricacies by recognizing your thoughts, feelings, actions and reactions.

Explore the following questions in your journal:

> What are my trigger times: After work? After dinner? On the commute home? Watching TV?

- ➤ Do I overeat at restaurants? With friends? At my mom's house? When I am alone?
- ➤ Do I find myself bingeing because I am ravenous, tired, depressed, bored, worried, angry or conversely happy and excited and use food to celebrate?
- ➤ Do I overeat when I drink alcohol? Smoke pot?
- ➤ What do I need to do to decrease the likelihood of bingeing?

I know the end of the workday is one of my trigger times; my thoughts are turning to food. I am biologically hungry and dreaming about what is for dinner while worrying if I can make it until then without eating. As the fear, created by my feelings of hunger grows, my thoughts become obsessive. If I buy jalapeño potato chips on the way home from work, (craving the spice, salt and crunch and ultimately the distraction from the day's events), scarf them down secretly in my car, although pleasant and satisfying during the act, within ten minutes after finishing I feel thirsty and slightly nauseous. It only took me ten years to figure this out! I now make sure I have other snacks around, ones that agree with me and don't cause me indigestion. I spend a few moments eating the food before I get into the car in order to give the snack my full attention. I have also learned to relax with the feelings of hunger. When I do decide to have my beloved potato chips, I am not just shoving them down in a post-work panic. I try to give the potato chips the attention they deserve so I can really enjoy them and discern when I have had enough.

Decide what you need to address and what specific changes you want to make. Banish the phrase 'I was good today' from your vocabulary. This is not about good or bad, it is about seeing your own process. This phase is about getting curious and increasing awareness of self, and planning accordingly. It is not about following someone else's imposed diet rules.

Making food choices and deciding what kind of gas to put in the tank is a four-part process:

HUNGER

PORTIONS

TASTE AND SATIATION

NUTRITIONAL QUALITY

1. Hunger: You're Not Starving, You're Just Hungry

Food addicts rarely feel real biological hunger because we make sure we get enough to eat. Conversely, food addicts often believe they are hungry, because we mistake feelings of hunger for other feelings. Learning to put up with some biological hunger is a way to start to discern the difference.

Most of the advice from diet experts reinforces the fear of hunger. Weight-loss books have built in snack plans, what we should eat between meals, before dinner, tricks to make sure we stave off that hunger. There is an inherent message that being hungry is not okay, that we can't handle it. But in truth we can. Human beings are designed to fear hunger. It is a primal fear and we are programmed to react. On the other hand we are also built to be able to tolerate hunger; in fact being hungry is one of many natural human states. We are designed to use up excess nutrients from the store rooms of our body to save us in times of starvation as we have seen countless times in history.

I am not suggesting we learn to starve ourselves. No healthy human being would do that intentionally. But when we realize we can handle a certain amount of hunger and learn to stop ourselves from eating at the first hunger pain, this creates an opportunity to build up some tolerance. Hunger triggers fear and food addicts believe the only way to stop the fear is to eat. This is untrue; you do not have to eat.

Practice. Remember food addicts are afraid of their hunger, and like many human fears, it is irrational. Strike the statement 'I'm starving' from your vocabulary. You are not starving. You are just hungry. The more we practice facing our fears the quicker they dissipate. Spend one day or half a day eating nothing. Start at breakfast and eat nothing else until dinnertime, or eat nothing when you get up until mid afternoon. Both suggestions assume you have no health issues. This gives you an opportunity to experience what it feels like to go for all those hours without food.

I found this suggestion in Judith Beck's book, *The Beck Diet Solution*, when she talked about building up a resistance habit.[2] I went from breakfast to dinnertime and discovered that I was okay, I didn't faint and the world didn't come to an end. Sensations from mild to strong hunger would flow in and out through the day and my belief that not eating all day would be horrible and intolerable proved groundless. It was really no big deal. I was just hungry.

Again, I am not suggesting we learn to starve ourselves. I do not recommend making the preceding experiment a new habit. What I propose is that we get curious about our hunger, take note of what we feel, the thoughts those feelings create, and our reactions. The experiment provided an excellent opportunity to face my fear with intent.

At times, especially when I am less conscious and find myself feeling really hungry it stresses me out, scares me and I have to work much harder to manage my fear and be with the hunger. Remember, we live in an environment where hunger can be easily satiated at any time. There is really nothing to fear. But your gut does not know that, your gut is operating on a primal instinct to get fed. You, as the guardian of your gut need to turn toward it and soothe it.

Take a moment, put your feet on the floor, take a deep breath and put your hand on your stomach, the place of discomfort. Breathe. Talk to it, silently or aloud, and quiet the fear. Tell it, you're okay, you're just hungry, it's okay. Give your fear conscious, loving messages that acknowledge the pain in order to keep the panic down. Tell yourself there is nothing to panic about. You are not waiting for your mate to bring home an antelope. You have food in the fridge, in the cupboard, at the restaurant and in the store. You are safe. Learning to tolerate, accept and be with our hunger takes that scary monster out o f the closet and into the light of day. It exposes the monster for what it is—just hunger.

Now that you have learned some strategies to be less fearful of your hunger, you can start to turn toward your hunger with curiosity instead of worry. Start noticing your levels of hunger and fullness by using a scale from 0 to 10 to grade your hunger. Record the score in your journal until you know it instinctively. The scale is from 0 (really famished) to 10 (stuffed to discomfort).[3] This tool will also help you to get better at discerning between real hunger and other feelings and figure what those other feelings are.

Tracking this carefully in your journal (again for a minimum of two weeks) will help you decide which numbers work for you. If you realize that letting your hunger slip below 3 sets you up for binge eating, adjust that number to 3.5 or 4 and get something to eat. This is an individual process of trial and error, there is no right or wrong. Once you commit, you will become more intuitive to your own signals of hunger and fullness; the process will become more natural. I try not to let my hunger level go below 2. If it does my stress levels increase and I am likely to eat more than I need. It is not about whether I 'should' be hungry; I just notice that I am, and I feed myself—a snack or a meal, depending on the time of day and when I know I will be eating next.

It is challenging to a food addict to not eat past our assigned fullness number, regardless of the tastiness of the food. Trying to stop before you stuff yourself and eat more than you physically need takes a high level of awareness.

There are theories that propose that we are better off eating frequently, but smaller portions. Eating frequent small meals throughout the day keeps our metabolism running faster, our machine running more efficiently. This method has served me well; when I am hungry, I try to eat enough to satiate that hunger, then eat again when I become hungry later. But a central aspect to this system is allowing myself to fully feel that hunger, not run and eat as soon as I get the first growl in my belly. Letting the hunger get to a 3, or even a 2 gives me a chance to be with the feeling, not to panic. The idea is to soothe it and be sure it actually is hunger. This part is an important step in learning to face the fear that hunger creates inside a food addict, and realizing that it is no big deal. It is just hunger.

Again, each of us needs to decide if this makes sense. Some people report that when they eat frequent, small meals they end up eating more than they normally would. Only you can decide what works for you.

2. Portions

We are truly a nation of pigs. The amount of food most folks in wealthy countries eat is ridiculous. Look at the size of the meals that come out of the kitchens of North American restaurants. It is enough food for the whole day! Who truly needs the 'lumberjack' breakfasts, except maybe a lumberjack? Three eggs, three rashers of bacon, three sausages, hash browns, and pancakes slathered with syrup and whipped cream, with a pathetic slice of orange on the side, topped off with twelve ounces of orange juice and three coffees. That amount of food is totally unnecessary, yet has become the accepted norm.

Liz Neporent, the author of a dozen fitness bestsellers points to the seminal American cookbook, The Joy of Cooking, which has been reprinted regularly since the 1930's, as an example of the normalcy of our increased portion sizes. Liz notes that a brownie recipe from a 1960's edition was to serve 30 but in the current edition the exact same recipe suggested serving is sixteen![4] Explains a lot, doesn't it?

Obviously, we eat more than our body needs, or we wouldn't be fat. More goes in than is burned off. The National Weight Control Registry, an ongoing research study that tracks people who have lost weight and kept it off, reports that portion control is the number one strategy in keeping weight off. Therefore, until you can trust yourself to recognize and stop eating when you are full, experiment with ordering half-size portions at restaurants. Get the server to wrap up half your sandwich as soon as you order it. A tuna sandwich at a deli typically uses double the mayonnaise and tuna than most people would at home and often comes on thickly sliced bread. It is far more food than anyone physiologically needs. Make a decision to eat less before you are seduced by the delicious taste. The result is you will be nicely satiated instead of stuffed to an 8 or 9 on your hunger scale.

Use smaller plates and bowls when eating at home. If you are dishing up a bowl of chili, use a one-cup scoop. Try to take a break for at least five minutes to gauge your fullness before going back for a second helping. We are rarely, if ever, biologically hungry for more food. Second helpings are about so much more: the taste of the food, our habit of eating way too much, the fear of not having enough, being unable to sense our fullness, our inability to be present while we are eating, the desire to compliment the cook and/or the ingrained fear of waste. Waiting for five minutes allows you to get more in touch with those reasons and learn to manage them.

Planning and setting up the meal to accommodate smaller portions are habits to develop which will increase our awareness and ultimately end our addictive behaviors. Attending to our emotional selves will sustain those habits, and again, our journal can help with that work.

3. Tastes and Satiation

For goodness sake, don't eat food you don't like! We are fortunate to have an incredible variety of wonderful foods at our fingertips, so eat the foods you like, or, better yet, eat the foods you love. Experiment. Get lots of variety. Play with herbs. Take a cooking course. Find restaurants that cook with fresh ingredients. Have fun creating your own delicious meals, that leave you feeling satiated, not just physically, but emotionally as well. If you want filet mignon covered in Béarnaise sauce, yet order the poached salmon because you 'should', you may be setting yourself up for the late-night trip to the freezer for a tub of Haagen-Dazs. Order the steak, enjoy the richness of the meal, eat it slowly, savor every bite and leave some on your plate if you're full. Eating this meal won't hurt you and it won't make you fat. Eating mindlessly, shoveling food down when you are not hungry, grabbing handfuls of M&Ms every time you walk by the candy dish, and even eating too much of high-test foods like cherries or grapes way past the point of satiation is what makes you fat.

4. Nutritional Quality

Does this food make you feel good, put color in your cheeks, make your body run efficiently? Are you burping and farting, feeling bloated, having heart burn and/or headaches, make five trips to the bathroom, or worse, no trips? Do you feel desperate for a nap in the middle of the day? Do you wake up feeling hung-over? Trust your body to tell you the answers you need. If you have never looked at it this way, get out that journal and start exploring. Start noticing how different foods affect you. Certain reactions could indicate an undiagnosed illness such as diabetes, high blood pressure or food allergies. If you have suspicions, your doctor and/ or alternative healers, such as a Naturopath, can help confirm them. If your stomach is 'cast iron' and nothing much seems to affect you, look more carefully; notice your energy levels, skin health, the shine of your hair, your moods or emotional state, your ability to concentrate, even your skin smell, the taste in your mouth and how your breath smells. I make the assumption that most chronic dieters know something about nutrition; if you need help, get yourself a copy of Canada's Food Guideline or the guidelines of the country you live. These guidelines have been researched and proven to promote good health, which includes weight control, and are part of disease prevention. Healthy food guidelines are not the law, and nobody is going to arrest you if you do not follow them exactly. Just post them on your fridge door and keep them in mind when planning your menus.

The Second Step—Be With Your Food

There are endless ways that we addicts who profess to love food miss the true enjoyment of eating. When we are preoccupied with the day's events, planning the next moment, not fully in the present, we give neither our food nor ourselves the love and respect deserved. Smell, sight, texture or flavor are hardly noticed as we wolf it down, ignoring such basic body cues as the feeling of satiation.

I can hear many of you protesting, What is she saying, I enjoy my food, I love my food, I notice my food, that is my problem. I too have enjoyed many a wonderful meal, savoring each and every bite, and that behavior has not led me to be overweight. What has led me there is the mindless eating that happens at other times: dipping the crusty bread repeatedly into the spaghetti sauce and chowing down while I waited for the pasta to boil. By the time I got to the table, five chunks later, I was full, but it would have been impossible to not eat with my family. I did not let myself acknowledge the behavior. A piece of my mind had registered it, but I quieted that voice with my denial tactics.

Practice and learn to be present with food. Honor yourself by taking the time to choose and enjoy. Eating smaller becomes easy when we choose to eat the foods we love, and learn to be present with our food. Slowing down also promotes healthy digestion, giving our stomach enzymes the chance to do their job. The more we slow down, the more we are with the experience, the more likely it is that we will stop eating when we are full. We will actually eat less because we are emotionally and biologically satiated.

Commit to eating without distractions.[5] Give yourself permission to take the time to get pleasure from the food you have decided to eat. This sounds simple but for food addicts this is a radical shift. Our new relationship with food demands that we become more intimate and in the moment. This won't happen if you are distracted reading the back of the cereal box!

I still find it a struggle to remain present and aware and not slot in another task while eating lunch in my office. It takes all my resolve to stay with the experience. The computer pulls me, I need to answer my messages. I have limited time—my excuses are typical. My lunch was something to get through. Yet, how could a delicious piece of leftover pizza, homemade, covered in roasted vegetables and feta, be something to get through?

Commit to not eating while engaged in the following activities:

➢ Watching TV
➢ Working on the computer
➢ Driving or sitting in the car—ban the drive-through lunch!
➢ Watching a movie in a theatre
➢ Talking on the phone
➢ Taking part in a heated debate
➢ Standing and preparing food at the kitchen counter
➢ Standing, period.

Also, it is a good practice not to eat when you are experiencing a big emotion, whether it is positive or negative. Anger, feelings of stress along with good feelings like excitement and elation take us out of the moment. We may find ourselves eating quickly, popping bites in without notice, laughing, gabbing, having a great time, but eating way more than we intended or needed and not really tasting the food.

Note: Give yourself permission to bend the 'don't eat without distractions' rule at certain times. Popcorn at the movies or in front of the TV <u>occasionally</u> is one of those times for me. And sometimes I eat something on my drive home because for me that is better than coming in the door really hungry. But be conscious of your decision, and make eating with distraction an exception, not the norm.

The Handful Shuffle

Watch for the food addict's favorite dance, the 'handful shuffle'. Classic distracted eating. Handfuls of nuts, chips, dried cereal, cherries, candies, trail mix, whatever is around. Handfuls that are not appreciated, not fully tasted, just gobbled mindlessly as we go about our day-to-day routines. It has been suggested that we eat up to 25% of our daily calories mindlessly snacking. Wow, that's a lot of extra, unaccounted for calories! When I started looking at my own behavior I found this to be true.

And let's not forget the bites. The tasting while cooking, legitimate to a point, regularly goes far beyond. The forkful of cake while making a cup of tea, a spoonful of ice cream while getting the meat out of the freezer for dinner, finishing up what is left on the kids plate. There are endless ways of consuming calories (that add up) because of our chronic lack of presence

Other Food Choices

What about those other foods, the ones not mentioned in our food guides? Of course you are allowed to eat them and enjoy them. Remember, they are not forbidden. No food is forbidden unless you have a health issue and are directed by your doctor, or you decide to forbid it because eating it makes you feel physically bad or sets you up to engage in your addiction.

Certain foods, especially when you are learning how to manage your addiction, may be difficult to have around. If you love potato chips but are unable to eat a few without downing the whole bag, (which is actually the vast majority of us) leave them out of your life for now. You can eat them later when the tools to handle your addiction are gainfully employed. I try hard not to touch chips, my husband's favorite snack. I like them too, they are not my favorite snack but because they are always around, I start eating them. They make me fat because I overeat them. This is not banishment. I am not depriving myself. I have made a conscious choice and can change my mind at any time.

Use caution when buying low fat or diet food. Low fat does not necessarily mean better for you. A low fat substitute, something that has ten, 27 letter, unpronounceable words in the ingredient list should alert your attention. When you decide to eat something you desire, some food that is not in the food guide, like a fatty sweet dessert, make sure that it lives up to your expectations and satisfies your desires, that it does not compromise on taste, and is not filled with artificial chemicals in order to reduce calories. You deserve better. If cheesecake is your favorite dessert and you don't like the low fat version, eat the full fat one. Once you learn to trust yourself and have learned to eat intuitively, it will be easy to look at the cheesecake, decide if you really want it, sit down without distractions, cut a piece, taste it, savor it, and eat as much or as little of the piece as you want. Eating the cheesecake becomes about taste and satiation. You won't need to gobble down more than you want to once you release yourself from guilt and judgment.

YOUR BODY IS NOT A GARBAGE CAN!

I know this seems wasteful, especially to us 'lick-that-plate-clean' folks, but it is better to throw something out rather than apply it mindlessly to your middle. Many of us have been trained to finish everything on our plate by previous generations who experienced scarcity of food and wasted nothing. This behavior is very difficult to deprogram, yet breaking out of that pattern is extremely important. We have enough food. We are not living in post-war Germany; we are not living through a famine in Africa. The sad truth is, throwing away food that your body does not need does not affect those less fortunate. It just adds weight. The optimal solution when you decide you are full is to put the left over food away, freeze the extra portions or give it away to friends, family, co-workers, a soup kitchen or the food bank. If this is not possible, difficult as it may be, throwing food away is a preferable option than using your body as a garbage disposal.

You have enough! Believing that you have enough food, attention, money, love—is about living in the moment and being okay with where you are in that instant. Throw out the second half of the brownie if you don't want it. You will be fine. The world won't come to an end. Be in charge of what you eat by taking back your power over food.

Alcohol

Many food addicts love their booze, especially wine. This may be an innocent enjoyment or another addiction. It may be time for you to have an honest look at that too. If you are not addicted but like a drink, becoming more aware of your alcohol consumption is important because drinking, even a little, decreases inhibitions and sets us up for overeating. Let's face it, after a couple of glasses of wine, who cares? So as with all your favorite foods, enjoy your drink of choice, but remember that too much alcohol is not a gift to your body, it is high in calories and has minimal, if any nutritional value and it increases the likelihood you will overeat.

*   *   *

Listening to our bodies and knowing what is the best fuel for our engines takes time, effort and trust in the self. Trust in the self is a difficult concept in these days of the 'expert'. There is always someone telling us what is right or wrong, what we should or shouldn't believe or do. Yet becoming your own expert is the smartest, most realistic endeavor possible. You know your body better than anyone. And if you do not, now is the time to learn. We have an inner guide, always there to access, one we can actually learn to follow. What is right for you nutritionally is at your fingertips; actually it is within you, buried in your innate senses. The first thing that needs to happen is to believe truly that food is not your enemy. Make peace with food. Food is just food. Take your power back. When we make peace with food and throw down our weapons—our diet books and calorie counters and quiet the diet police in our head—we will be embracing a tremendous paradigm shift. A shift where we learn to trust our body's signals, instead of following someone else's external rules. Start hearing what your body is saying. It is the right time to gently create a new relationship with food that is based on testing, listening, and honoring your body without judgment, and without unrealistic weight-loss deadlines. This is the start of a new love affair, one in which you get to know yourself, the essence of you, regardless of what's happening outside your door.

Questions and Contemplations to Explore in Your Journal

1. Do you find yourself still trying/reading the latest diet fads, looking for the answer?

2. Do you look at food in terms of good and bad?

3. Do you eat things you don't like because you believe it is 'good for you' or the 'right' way to eat?

4. Do you really know how much you consume in an average day?

5. If you were not aware, what would be your plan to increase awareness?

6. Do you know what your trigger times are to overeat?

7. Are there certain foods that you have a hard time not bingeing on?

8. Do you know the difference between real hunger and other emotions?

9. Do feelings of hunger scare you?

10. What does the idea of being with or really feeling your hunger pains feel like to you?

11. What do you think you need in order to be able to manage feelings of hunger without panicking?

12. Do you consider yourself someone who eats fast?

13. Do you eat without distractions?

14. If not, what percentage of the time would you say that you do eat without distractions?

15. What do you need to do to increase that?

"Body loathing – what has it cost me? I could have taken off my shorts and worn a bathing suit in swim class; I could have had more fun building sandcastles with my daughters, I missed out on a lot of fun, with my friends, husband and my children while they were toddlers, I held back because I hated my body so much."[1]

Anonymous 200
Ways to Love the Body You Have

CHAPTER SIX

———

Exercise You Got To Move It-Move It!

As PROMISED, I am not going to spend a lot of time on the subject of exercise but I cannot leave it out entirely, since exercise is an important part of being healthy. At the risk of stating the obvious, exercise has numerous benefits: Exercise builds a stronger heart, prevents disease, especially diabetes and high blood pressure, improves mental function, helps elevate our moods, increases energy, improves sex life, helps us manage our stress levels and aids with sleep. In short, exercise improves all areas of our lives. And exercise makes us feel good about our bodies, regardless of our weight.

Dr. Arya Sharma, the scientific director of Canadian Obesity Network, is quoted in a 2010 article in Maclean's magazine by

Kate Lunau stating that, "Exercise has lots of health benefits, but losing weight is not one of them."[2] After you pick yourself up off the floor, spend a moment to think about her statement. When I first heard this information I felt a mixture of shock that was quickly followed by relief. I have exercised for years, done a triathlon, some ten kilometer running races, a half marathon and participated in various programs that were pretty intense workouts. I have enjoyed all my athletic pursuits immensely and I do believe it has kept my weight from getting higher than it has, exercise alone has never led me to lose any substantial weight. When I was in my twenties, ten pounds would fall off, but now, in my fifties I may only go down about four. Not much weight when I look at my level of activity. My standard joke was I would have to put a stick of dynamite up my behind to lose five pounds!

Not losing the weight while engaged in these pursuits did not stop me. I love exercise for the camaraderie, and the way it makes my body feel. I walk taller, feel stronger, feel generally happier and I have more energy. While I tried to accept my 'slow metabolism', or whatever I attributed it to, I was frustrated and bewildered. It never quite made sense to me.

The truth of the statement, 'exercise does not make one lose weight', comes back to simple math. To lose weight there must be a caloric deficit. If one eats exactly the same amount of calories (not the controlled behavior of a food addict) and adds exercise, weight loss will happen. If one reduces calories and exercises, weight will happen faster. But if beer and nachos at the pub follows the Thursday night game of squash with the boys, there isn't going to be any weight loss. The 300 calories you burnt at the squash game just got gobbled up and then some.

Realistically, if one decided to become an ultra marathoner weight loss would occur. Athletes are rarely fat, are usually very careful about what they eat and train extensively, clocking countless hours per week. If they are food addicts, the intensity and volume of exercise counters weight gain. Exercise or sport is their passion (possibly obsession); it is how they spend their time. It is what they do.

But For most of us mere mortals getting a workout at the gym, a walk, a bike ride or maybe an extra long hike on the weekend is as good as it gets. It is just not enough to budge the bulge if you don't reduce the food intake. The damn blubber wants to stay there and some people actually gain weight when they increase their exercise. Exercise does not decrease our appetites, another popular claim. Rather it stimulates our appetites and makes us hungrier and as we know, food addicts are not going to let an appetite go unfed.

An article in a 2007 issue of Time Magazine written by J. Cloud suggests that the current way we approach exercise itself is problematic. We drive to the gym to work out for an hour; drive to work and sit all day; drive home and sit on our butts for the rest of the evening. Obesity researchers now believe that frequent, low-level physical activity, the kind humans have done for thousands of years may actually do us more good than intense, sweaty workouts.[3]

So should we give up on the gym, the programs that promise to trim inches, increase muscle mass and make us leaner? Absolutely not! Group programs, even if it is just you and a personal trainer, decrease isolation, motivate us to keep moving and keep on track.

That same Time magazine article speaks of a study that examined the dynamics of a rowing team from Oxford University, researchers found that rowers who worked out together could tolerate twice as much pain as rowers who worked out alone. Researchers discovered that working out as a group increases endorphin levels, which not only promotes higher pain tolerance, but more importantly, contributes to heightened feelings of happiness and belonging, feelings all humans long for.[4] You may not be motivated to increase pain tolerance but group workouts do connect us and often become an important social network.

Make sure you love your workout. Don't drag your butt to spin class if you hate it. If you've always loved swimming, join a swim class. If you enjoy dancing, join a dance class and let go of how uncoordinated you are. I spent the eighties in aerobics class going the wrong way. But I showed up. If you pick something you love you won't be wasting your money. You won't, yet again, buy the ten-time pass to the workout you hate and drop out after three times. Find something you love by mixing it up. You aren't training to become a competitive swimmer. If you are sick of the swim class, take up tennis. Just get out there and try new things.

The shame of obesity keeps many people away from exercise, to embarrassed to go to the gym, participate in a group dynamic or even going for a walk. Body loathing keeps us isolated, hiding out. But today is the day you are in; it isn't about when you get there. Accept that and get moving. Exercise is a gift to yourself, a way to love yourself regardless of your weight today. Feel your heart pump, notice the blood flow through your veins and appreciate the rosy glow on your cheeks.

If you are significantly overweight please see a doctor before embarking upon an exercise program. This is the standard advice from any health care professional but it is scary how many people do not heed it. Feelings of embarrassment shame and disgust keep us underground and stop us from talking to the doctor. Obviously I need to lose weight, I'm fine, I'm just lazy, exercise won't hurt me, it is about time I got off my ass, just do it.

Jumping into an exercise program without consulting your doctor can be a deadly mistake. A dear friend, ashamed of her weight, convinced herself that the reason she was always so winded was the extra forty pounds she carried. Although there was truth in that argument, it turned out that she also had an undiscovered heart defect. A routine hike, one she had done many times proved to be her last. I implore you to go to your doctor and request the testing to make sure all is working as it should be.

Kick-start yourself. Do something outrageously fun; something that you have secretly wished for but never had the nerve. How about bike trip in the south of France, or a hike on the West Coast Trail on Vancouver Island? Why not try to walk up that hill at the end of your street instead of avoiding it. The world offers so many adventures; from safe, luxurious ones with all the trimmings (like a exercise spa), to hard-core and austere (like trail running). And walking and running is cheap. Embrace your inner athlete. You are designed to move. If your childhood did not involve climbing trees, doing cartwheels and running through sprinklers, it may have been your dream. You now have the ability to make that dream come true.

Get moving. Walk into town, park in the farthest corner of the parking lot, take a little stroll after dinner, climb up and down the stairs a dozen times instead of dangerously loading your laundry basket to save on steps. Spend them. Get out and weed that garden. For goodness sakes, shovel your driveway, cut your own grass and rake the leaves. Get rid of the leaf blower! Keep moving.

If we don't use it, we really will lose it. Strength, mobility, flexibility and balance are keys to physical health, especially healthy aging. But researchers from Northwestern University remind us that having a normal body mass is more important in preventing disease than being aerobically fit.[5] That means keeping your weight down. So start! Add or keep up with your exercise. Increase your daily movement for the benefits activity brings into your life. But most important, if you want to lose weight or maintain a healthy body weight, increase the awareness around what you are eating.

Questions and Contemplations to explore in Your Journal:

1. How often do you exercise?
2. Do you mix it up?
3. What is your idea of the perfect exercise for you?
4. How can you make that more challenging?
5. Who can you find to be an exercise buddy or motivator?
6. What excuses do you used, not to exercise?
7. How can you get rid of those excuses?

CHAPTER SEVEN

———

Spirituality: Encouraging Dialogue With the Soul

DEVELOPING A SPIRITUAL practice and figuring out what that truly means to each of us is vital to beating our food addiction. After all, ending a food addiction or any addiction is a spiritual journey. A journey that ultimately takes us home to ourselves. Addictions are a classic way to disconnect, we choose, consciously or unconsciously, not to hear what we really hunger for, what we really need.

Spirituality is about being with self, connecting to our core, some call our soul. It is about how conscious we are, how awake we are in our lives. Becoming conscious, being awake in the world is the opposite of addictive behavior. As addicts we look outwards, obsessively scrambling for the next hit. Addictions turn us away from ourselves. In order to beat our food addiction, we need to turn back. Addicts are looking for a way out of the trenches, the slog and mud we trudge through filled with fear and worries, and ascend to the quieter place that resides inside all of us. When we are connected spiritually we are in that place, we feel alert, alive and in the moment.

The extraordinary rise of obesity reflects a mass spiritual disconnection. Obesity rates have increased dramatically for all population groups in the United States, and most other western countries, over the last several decades. Statistics found on Wikipedia declare that between 1986 and 2000, the prevalence of severe obesity quadrupled from one in two hundred Americans to one in fifty.[1] Because of Western society's abundance, food is a viable way to fill the void disconnection creates. Overeating is just one facet of our gargantuan consumption. It has become apparent that we are starving for something else.

So how do we start connecting with that part which resides in all of us that as addicts we may have forgotten? How do we learn to fill ourselves up with something other than food? How do we learn to connect to our elusive soul?

It is about remembering. The feeling of spiritual connection is a fundamental human experience. We, addicts included, have all had this feeling at one point or another during our lives. It is that calm, that awe when starring out the window, silenced by the beauty of the first frost. It is the feeling of reverence when you receive the gift of watching a mother bear play with her cub. The tranquility one feels while engaged in prayer at a place of worship.

In those moments we feel peace, feel a connection to all living things, the noise in our head is quiet. We understand we are part of something larger. Are able to appreciate we are an integral piece and feel the significance of our worth.

When connected to ourselves we become fully aware of our existence but without ego. This is that mysterious state some call being in the now.[2] In this state we are not compelled to engage in our addictions, have a moment where the battle is suspended, our minds are still and we are with all that is, however fleeting.

Alcoholics Anonymous, still one of the most successful organizations for alcoholics, central concept is one of surrender 'to a higher power'. Because addictions are like being in combat, the notion of surrender is invaluable. Food addicts are in a relentless conflict, bingeing and berating, starting another diet, searching for the next best secret to end the war with food, lose the weight and stop the insanity. But we're not winning. So if we surrender in whatever way that means to each of us, we can let go and give in to the mysteries of life. We can quiet the ego, the place inside that berates us unmercifully, thinks it knows better, believes it should know all, believes it can find the answers, convinced it can control.

If we surrender and make ourselves open to possibilities there is an actual loosening of the grip we hold so tight, a liberation of our so-called truths. We can let go of the obsession about food and diets, the merry-go-round of the weight loss battle. It is about finding the capacity to be open and learn to trust there is something to discover within the quiet places of self. We become humble when we stop talking, doing, and thinking and start to listen. In this moment, we are, however fleeting, truly awake. For me, this is where I find my spiritual self.

I have seen from the experiences of my own life and the journey I take with clients each day that big and lasting change, by and large has a spiritual component. Find what that means to you.

Questions and Contemplations to Explore in Your Journal:

1. Do you have a concept of what spirituality means to you?
2. Do you know when you are in that place?
3. What are the signs?
4. Can you see that when you are engaging in your addiction that you are not embracing your spiritual self?
5. What does the concept of surrender mean to you?
6. How would you know if you have surrendered?
7. What do you need to do to increase your connection to self?

'Eat When You're Hungry, Sleep When You're Tired
and Cry When You're Sad.'

Zen Mantra

CHAPTER EIGHT

───────

Finding Your Centre:
The Mindful Way Home

A FEW YEARS ago I found myself sitting on a patio overlooking the ocean in Mexico, reading a book about Africa. The absurdity of the situation suddenly struck me. I laid my book aside and spent the better part of the next hour watching pelicans dive for their supper, the red sun slipping into the Pacific. Resting there, I could hear the cries of the birds, feel the breeze off the ocean, and smell the salt air mingle with the cooking smells coming from a nearby kitchen. My breathing was slow and rhythmic, my muscles relaxed and for a time, I felt glued to that spot.

The Buddhist concept of mindfulness is the practice of being intentionally aware and fully present in the moment. It is about noticing, without judgment, what is happening as it unfolds. Sitting on a Mexican patio drinking in the ocean's beauty should provide an easy place to practice this skill. But being mindful can elude us even in the loveliest settings.

The ability to be truly in your surroundings, to notice what you are thinking and feeling, see what you are doing and to be able to feel your breath go in and out takes a keen awareness. It is the capacity to be fully embodied, all five senses engaged instead of just being a walking head, obsessing on the latest problem or plan.

When I am mindful my world comes into focus. The frame freezes and I am present in the moment, however mundane. I literally lift my head up from my swirling thoughts and use the opportunity to stretch my mindful muscle. At home in the kitchen, I lift the large baking sheet that drains beside the sink. It feels cool and weighty in my hand as I slowly dry each section with a soft tea towel. I pay careful attention to each corner where water droplets rest, my arm moves in a circular rotation, wiping and stroking until the job is complete. I turn, open the drawer on the bottom of the oven and stack the pan underneath the others with care to not upset the fragile pyramid. While I keep my focus, I notice my breath slows in time with the purpose of my movements. I hear a bird, and remember it is spring. I perceive its movement out of the corner of my eye, through the kitchen window. There is a slight tingling in my chest, a feeling I link to the worry I carry about my mother's failing health. Nothing is right, nothing is wrong, it just is.

Becoming more mindful does not necessarily transform one into a smiling Buddha. Mindfulness is not always about witnessing the beauty of pelicans diving into a Pacific sunset. When we strive to become aware, the very things we try to avoid become highlighted. The feeling in my chest that I link to fear is inescapable when I am mindful. It is not a pleasant sensation but it carries important information about the anxieties I carry connected to my mother's health. My parents are aging and I see their decline. I live far away and I feel a sense of helplessness. Acknowledging my feelings allows me to make choices instead of reacting. One possible choice is to sit with the feelings, breathe through the discomfort and just notice it, acknowledge the reality that I can't change things.

Mindfulness is the ability to see clearly whatever is in front of us in the moment. Rumination, that chronic merry-go-round of thinking and worry that swirls in our heads is the antithesis of mindfulness. If we ponder long enough we will find a way to control the situation, then plan our way out of whatever is plaguing us. Our ego, with its arrogance and righteousness, or shame and self-pity, leads the charge. It knows who we should be and how we should act and how it should turn out. And it works, kind of, for a while, until the next time. I can berate my mother's doctor about his inability to fix her, I can read the latest medical information and find the best medication, and nag her to take better care of herself but her aging and deterioration advances regardless of my efforts. There are some things you cannot control.

Being more mindful is not about giving up on trying to sort things out. It is about giving up the innocent, naïve idea that if we can get away from painful things we will be happy. Real happiness, as the Buddhist nun Pema Chodron says in her work, *The Wisdom of No Escape and the Path of Loving Kindness*, "... comes from seeing clearly with precision and gentleness that right now this is the body we have, the mind we have, the domestic situation we have, the job we have and these are the people in our lives at present."[1] We can look for solutions and ways to change our circumstances while accepting that we are in pain and that things are the way they are.

In regards to your weight and relationship to food, you can use this clear seeing to be in the moment with gentleness and the Buddhist concept of 'loving-kindness'. Julie explains, "practicing mindfulness reminds me to love myself today, not when I lose the thirty pounds I need to lose and to be in the moment I am in, however painful, exciting, happy or otherwise it might be. As I have become more mindful, I have learned to tell the difference between emotional and physical hunger, something I had not distinguished between for a VERY long time. Now that I can see the difference, I can tell when I am craving food for emotional reasons. I am learning to tell myself that 'this food won't really help' . . . and ask myself, 'what do you really need'? I am able to take away the romanticized lure of food and see through the web of confused emotions and beliefs that has been my relationship with food. What is interesting to me is that as I give up trying to control everything I actually feel way more in control."

A simple translation of the first noble truth of Buddhism states that to be human is to suffer. This is not to be interpreted as a negative statement; it is meant to be seen as a basic, fundamental truth of human existence. Suffering, very simply put from a Buddhist standpoint, is created by what we crave and by the attachment we have to things, to people and to outcomes and is formed by our servitude to the ego. The ego is busy justifying and defending how things should or should not be; without the light of mindfulness it controls our actions, defends our hurts and looks for reassurance and accomplices.

I understand that my suffering is a choice. I realize that my old story suggested that I could never lose weight and keep it off; it was really not my fault, but the fault of slow metabolism and genetics. These tales kept me attached to my feelings of powerlessness. It is a story created by the victim and the judge that resides inside of me wrapped up in the arms of my ego. These stories feel like trusted friends. They are not.

Eckhart Tolle calls the ego our 'illusionary self'.[2] This 'self' we create consciously and unconsciously becomes our identity or what we think of as our personality. Some people will pronounce 'That's just the way I am', as though this illusionary self is a fixed, static state. Humans are far from static; in fact, my illusionary self, the portrait I paint, is the one thing I do have power over. Mindfulness is the key to that power. "All that is required to become free of the ego is to be aware of it, since awareness and ego are incompatible." Tolle continues, "Awareness is the power that is concealed within the present moment."[3]

When we get quiet and expose our latest, greatest version of our events, and start to see our story as coming from our illusionary self, a whole new world opens up. Linda's ego defiantly justified her addiction to sweets, particularly chocolate. Like a six-year-old saying 'you're not the boss of me', she took her power and stood her ground in an area that made no sense and did not enhance her life. By gorging on chocolate, Linda would show her deceased, alcoholic father and her abusive first husband that they could no longer control her. Her mindfulness practice changed things and allowed her "... to enjoy one piece of chocolate instead of the whole large bar, because eating the whole bar was not bringing pleasure to me like I pretended it did. Eating the whole bar did not 'fix' anything. Physically and spiritually I was creating my own pain and suffering."

The ego is tenacious and loves to rule the roost! I don't expect to be free of mine anytime soon. On a good day, I can see it conducting the orchestra of my divided selves, enjoying the limelight or sulking in the shadows, depending on the play du jour. In that instant of clarity I can be gentle with myself and relish the moment of insight; I can see what my ego is up to, and see it for what it is, an unconscious driving force intent on managing my fears. I can stand back and observe, 'oh you're on your third trip to the ice cream carton ... interesting ... what is going on with you? Oh, you want that contract so badly, it will mean you are recognized ... it's okay, you are enough; you are wonderful and just fine with or without that contract ... your stomach is churning, it's just fear. Remember—nothing is the end of the world'.

When I turn toward my self with loving-kindness and spot the ego, dancing its dance, I can gently lead it to a comfy chair. I can spend some time, sit and embrace the feelings that come up: the fears, the loneliness and the confusion. I am with my feelings and thoughts, allowing them the space and form they need to morph and move along, as they always do, like the clouds passing in a summer's sky. The one universal truth that is hard to dispute and is evident in all of nature is that everything changes and all is impermanent. 'This too will pass'.

As I sit quietly and surrender to the emotion that I label loneliness, and notice the quality of the feeling and where it resides in my body, the emotion starts to change. A sting forms behind my eyes and tears begin to well. There is a quiver in my lips and my chest feels tight. I let the feelings flow, trying not to judge or fix, just let them be. Nothing needs to be done. Turning toward my emotions with compassion creates a path for transformation. Anxiety is just anxiety. Pain is just pain. Discomfort is just discomfort.

When I stopped using food to manage my emotions, I noticed a marked increase in feelings of anxiety. Before bed, satiated or slightly hungry, a different state than my usual condition, stuffed with the evening munching, I had nothing to protect me from the burn that I felt in my chest, between my breastbones. The same burn I'd felt in the past, in times of stress. If I didn't use food, what stood between my feelings and myself? I was agitated, fearful and had a difficult time falling asleep, which are classic symptoms of giving up addiction. My thoughts created the fuel that I threw on the fire of my anxiety. My thoughts fanned the flames that built the inferno. I no longer had food to put it out.

Mindfulness became my new fire extinguisher, but it takes a lot more effort and awareness than eating spoonfuls of ice cream. Learning to sit without judgment and let the wave of feeling wash over me is scary. I hate that burn. It terrifies me and takes me back to past traumas. Sometimes the feeling is so strong it is almost overwhelming. I had to learn to lean into the discomfort. This place inside of me is not a beast after all. It is a scared part of me. I had to learn that 'anxiety is just anxiety'. I had to learn to trust the breath. Paying attention to the breath is the most basic way to bring focus into the body. Settle into the rhythm. By bringing awareness into the body, we can leave the craziness of our head, the swirling non-stop chaotic babble of the ego.

Mind chatter, and the resulting feelings of anxiety, is rarely pathological or a true mental illness. It is just the worries and stresses of life. Yet for some, the strength of emotion evoked is extremely difficult to sit with. Whether strong emotion or relatively benign, the feelings created from that mind-babble precede addictive behavior.

On Mike's journey to become mindful he realized that he was at a point in his life where, "There was nothing that I was compensating for—just a vague anxiety that would evaporate when I took a look at it. It was almost the reverse—the habit of soothing with food was so ingrained that I created the anxiety in order to soothe it. In any event, there was really nothing there, but what I had to understand and then create, was the habit of stopping and asking myself why I was reaching for whatever it was that I was reaching for."

Tools To Promote Mindfulness

Meditation

Mindfulness is a practiced skill and meditation is the key to the practice. Much has been written about meditation; too much for this work but I will attempt to share a few key points that hopefully will pique your interest to investigate further. Meditation is an intentional path to get quiet, go within and develop a deeper relationship with self. This ritual has been practiced for thousands of years, by many traditions, the most common being Buddhism. Western societies are slowly awakening to what Eastern societies have known for centuries—meditation is good for you. The scientific evidence supporting the health benefits is overwhelming. "Through simple shifts in attention and intention, meditators are able to slow their heart rates, reduce their breathing patterns, and lower their blood pressure.", writes David Simon and Deepak Chopra in *Freedom From Addiction* "They can reduce their levels of stress hormones and create coherent brain waves."[4]

Dr. Daniel Siegel, a leading expert who links brain science to the practice of psychotherapy, talks about the elasticity of the brain and its ability to change. He explains the innate human concept of attunement as the ability to channel our attention, and how this channeling leads to healthy growth of the prefrontal fibers. The middle prefrontal regions, a place in the brain that connects other functions, and are so important to our healthy functioning, are thicker in mindful practitioners than in the general population. His work reveals that the practice of mindfulness helps the parts of the brain that regulate our mood to grow and strengthen, which stabilizes the mind and enables greater emotional equilibrium and resilience.[5]

For many, the idea of incorporating a meditation practice into their daily life seems like a waste of time. For years I was resistant to the very word 'meditation', I saw it as some woo-woo weird practice that seemed pointless. I was not prepared to make the sacrifice to sit still, the opposite of North American 'get things done' zeitgeist, in the hope of some nebulous change that I didn't really understand. Yet there has to be something to this if people worldwide have been practicing meditation for thousands of years, people who did not need modern science to confirm what they knew from experience.

Like every other skill we attempt to master, the more we practice, the greater the results. At a retreat I asked my teacher how many minutes a day one should meditate, he answered, ". . . well you know, we want to get into shape, we buy a membership to the gym, we go five minutes, three times and week and we are doing more exercise than we did before . . ." Obviously it's going to take a long time at that rate. And yet from a Buddhist perspective, I remind myself to remain detached from outcome. I am not trying to get a gold star in meditating. I just need to sit.

So I try to do a daily practice of twenty minutes sitting, although many days it does not happen, I avoid it like the plague. I don't totally get it, I don't feel hugely different and to be honest, I would rather read a magazine. But I am committed because some slight change does happen when I sit. For those brief moments I am quieter and I do notice what is happening inside. There is a softening, a loosening of all I am holding tight. There is a silence I can't explain but it feels fundamentally important, on a primitive level, to my well-being. I have had fleeting experiences of connecting to that level and I want more. I walk away from my meditation practice quieter yet, alert. I notice what is happening around me and feel a general increase in awareness.

The work at the Chopra Center for Wellbeing has led Simon and Chopra to conclude that meditation is the key to changing negative, addictive patterns. They propose meditating fifteen to twenty minutes twice a day.[6] That being said, many people wonder how to get started.

The simplest practice is as follows: find a quiet spot, sit in a chair, back straight, feet planted firmly on the floor, hands resting on thighs, palms down, or rest a hand on your heart or stomach if that brings comfort, then simply start breathing deeply, in through the nose, out through the mouth. Concentrate on the breath coming in, expanding the lungs. Follow where the breath travels. Take note of where you feel your breath coming and going; is it the cool breeze above your lip, or the expansion of your chest or the rise and fall of your stomach? Let your eyes rest in front of you, slightly downward. Feel yourself relax into the breath without judgment. If uncomfortable feelings arise, breathe into them and let them pass. Remind yourself that it is just a feeling.

To sit and just be aware and focus on the breath coming in and out is almost impossible for the beginner meditator. Even long term meditators struggle. Your mind will wander all over the place, grab ideas and thoughts, bring them into focus, follow threads of stories. This is perfectly normal. Just say 'thinking' to yourself and bring your awareness back to the breath. Be patient. Do not judge or criticize. You are in the beginning stages of a meditation practice. How far you develop your practice, what you learn, which tradition you follow is yet to be known. But for today just sit for a time and breathe.

I embarked upon a meditation practice to end my food addiction and found success. Learning to be quiet and hear what I needed was a key component in my recovery. However, from a Buddhist perspective the core of meditation practice is not intended to be self-serving. For my spiritual growth, I decided to re-define my intent. After a period of reflection, I expanded the objective of my meditation practice to a less self-serving goal: 'to decrease my judgment of self and others while increasing my compassion'. This path is about letting go of fear and bringing in love, because judgment is a function of fear and compassion is a function of love. What happened to me is that the harried cravings of addiction fell away.

The path of mindfulness leads to a greater acceptance of human frailty in all its form. It is okay if I eat more than I plan to now and then. If I slip into a binge my job is to spend more time uncovering the 'why' of the binge and to spend little or no time scolding. My task is to learn to accept the flaws in my mother's care when appropriate, accept the reality of her failing health and her aging, and to trust that people are doing the best they can. I touch my fear with compassion; say kind things to it, because I know I can't always control the fear with outside actions. I invite fear in with the Buddhist mantra, 'Hello fear, I know you're there, come in for a cup of tea'. I don't need to distract myself with food.

Learning, and committing to a meditation practice is like learning anything else in life, you need to find your own way. Do not be afraid to experiment. You can learn to meditate by downloading a guided meditation and putting it on your iPod. There are numerous books available on meditation and CDs offering guided meditations. Many North American communities have meditation groups that meet regularly, folks who have found the benefit and are thrilled to share it with others. There are many wonderful teachers who are eager to impart their knowledge and wisdom.

More Ways To Be Meditative

You might start by formalizing the way you stare out your window at your favorite view, in silence, being conscious and noticing the thoughts that drift in and out. Or you may start by committing to spending ten minutes each morning in that same spot with a cup of tea, without checking your email or reading a magazine. Mindfully being with the cup of tea with no distractions. The next time you take a walk notice your feet hitting the ground, your breathing, the smells and the sounds. You can chant quietly 'heel, toe, heel, toe, heel, toe.' That is the start of formalizing a walking meditation, another way to increase awareness.

The benefits of meditation are indisputable, yet some of you may be thinking 'it's never gonna happen . . . When is she going to stop going on about this? . . . I just don't see myself doing that.' If this is you, don't worry about it. Just commit to trying something new, something that is meditative, repetitive and trance-like. Most of us are fortunate enough to have access to many interesting disciplines, even if it means popping in a DVD. It is a matter of exploring and choosing something that feels right.

Yoga is wonderful. Try a variation that is gentle, meditative and spiritual rather than one that teaches you how to lift and hold your body weight on your forearms. Tai Chi, another ancient art that is often described as a moving meditation, cultivates tranquility by doing very specific, slow and repetitive exercises. And there are newer practices such as Nia, an exercise program set to music that combines dance, martial and healing arts, which is designed for personal growth and benefits the body, mind and spirit.

There is more than one way to increase mindfulness; however, moving meditations do not replace sitting meditations. Movement distracts because we are following instructions, striving to get it right, keeping our balance, keeping in rhythm. Sitting meditation offers a stillness that is hard to replicate. But moving meditations or mini quiet times like being with your tea are viable alternatives, can be used as add-ons to a mediation practice, and are definitely superior to no meditation at all. So get started, explore and find something that becomes part of your life.

Don't worry if you have trouble doing any kind of sitting or keeping still. You may be at the beginning of your healing journey and are completely unable to stay still. Your body may carry too much trauma energy that needs to be discharged. This is not a negative reflection on you, it just means you may want to do some more inner work before you can get to a place of stillness in your life.

Body Breaks

Incorporate simple body breaks into your day. By this I mean spending a minute, at least three times a day, breathing deeply, and noticing all that is present at that moment. You can do a simple ten breaths in through the nose and ten breathes out through the mouth. Or you can practice different styles of breathing, like Pranayana breathing, a yoga practice of alternate nostril breathing. Yogis believe that this clears and rejuvenate your energy channels. It is also believed that this style of breathing produces optimum functioning and helps keep us balanced because as it accesses both sides of the brain.

To practice Pranayana breathing, sit with your two feet firmly planted on the floor cover your right nostril with your right thumb and breath into your left nostril to the count of four. Then cover the left nostril with your ring finger of the same hand and breathe out to the count of eight with your right nostril. Now breathe in with the right nostril, then breathe out with the left. This completes one round. Do three in a row and build up to seven.

When you are finished your breathing or your body break, whichever way you decide to do it, get out your journal and ask yourself three questions.

"What do I feel?" (physically, viscerally)
"What is that?" (one or two words)
"What do I need?"

Example:
"What do I feel?"—I feel a heaviness in my body. I feel stinging behind my eyes. I feel my heart low and weighty in my chest."
"What is that?"—"Sadness and fear."
"What do I need?"—Nothing, I need to just sit with it for a few minutes, I know what it is about (sometimes I don't and that is okay), I will just let the feeling wash over me and continue to breathe.
Another time I may need to call a friend or to have a good cry.

Notice: Get curious. Don't judge. Taking a moment and doing some breathing and checking in is a really useful exercise to do just before you eat. This is a specific, tangible way to practice getting in touch with your feelings so you can learn to feed yourself what you truly need. These breathing exercises give you that much needed time to transition from your busy life and swirling thoughts to stilling the mind with intention so that you can be present with your food.

Breathe. If you find a feeling or a thought that brings discomfort, talk to yourself in a soothing and loving way. Create some mantras that are filled with loving-kindness and forgiveness. Tell yourself that you know how to soothe yourself. You are all right. You are full. You are safe and you can handle your emotions. Just notice and let go. Try to pop a pin in the balloon of your fear stories. Let go of your worries and self-imposed judgment. Feel what you feel and let go. As difficult as this may be, when you learn to sit with the feelings and let the waves of what you perceive as unpleasant wash over, you may find acceptance, and ultimately, some peace and calm. As you become more mindful, you realize that it truly 'is what it is', and 'wherever you go, there you are'. And sometimes that is a really uncomfortable, painful place to be.

I like to think my goal to become more mindful is noble and for the greater good. In reality, my reasons are probably more self-serving than I admit. I regularly get off track and find myself back hanging with my ego, commiserating about my petty worries and complaints. The difference is, I have learned to forgive myself. Most times.

Pema Chodron quotes a teaching from Trungpa Rinpoche, in her book *The Wisdom of No Escape*, that speaks to our ego illusion. "You are never going to get it all together, you're never going to get your act together, fully, completely. You're never going to get all the little loose ends tied up."[7]

Life is messy and humans are flawed and for every moment that is tragic there are a thousand that are amazing.

Breathe.

Questions and Contemplations to explore in Your Journal:

1. Does the concept of mindfulness make sense to you?
2. Do you see how you could become more mindful?
3. Do you meditate now?
4. If yes, what do you notice?
5. If no, do you see how it could be useful?
6. What would you need to get started?
7. What would get in the way?
8. Will you commit to doing something meditative?

CHAPTER NINE

It Takes a Smorgasbord to Beat an Addiction

AT THIS POINT I hope it is evident that beating food addiction for good involves picking from a wide range of external and internal strategies. Lets summarize what we have learned:

- ➤ We now have a greater understanding regarding the root of our food addiction.
- ➤ We recognize other behaviors we engage in as potentially addictive.
- ➤ We have learned to hear and understand our inner voices.
- ➤ We have made some links to how we got into this dysfunctional relationship with food.

> ➢ We have learned some ways to get out of our unconscious behavior.
> ➢ We now understand somewhat the concept of mindfulness.
> ➢ We have learned how to meditate.
> ➢ We have slowed down our eating.
> ➢ We make more conscious choices.
> ➢ We see ourselves during a binge, and have had some success stopping and walking away.
> ➢ We have learned how to soothe ourselves.
> ➢ We have had success stopping the binge in mid-bite, and turn toward our emotions with loving-kindness.
> ➢ We have learned how to tolerate hunger.

Relapse

What I have learned for certain from years as a therapist, and through my own personal experience, is that anyone embarking upon giving up an addiction will slip. Therapists plan for that reality and weave it into the sessions (no matter how determined or excited our client may be about their newfound success). Never is this more relevant than when dealing with food addictions simply because we have to eat. And on occasion you will eat more than you intend. It may happen on a camping trip, at the cottage, at a wedding, over Christmas, or at some such celebration, and does not necessarily constitute a true slip. You may have just eaten too much.

A true slip or relapse is using the old behavior to cope. A binge is in reaction to work stress, relationship stress and life stress in general. It is a response to feeling big emotions that you typically numb with food. You have peeled enough of the onion to see what you are doing, maybe not in the exact moment, but soon after. You are now able to dissect the behavior, find the source or the trigger of the binge and gently remind yourself that what you need to do is dust yourself off and get back on the mindful path of awareness.

Ending food addiction, losing weight and keeping it off for good takes a significant amount of dedication and commitment until it gets easier, and more habitual. After losing twenty pounds, Mike still works hard to remain mindful. He says he fears slipping into old habits of avoidance, and reflexive self-soothing by eating and drinking without awareness. "I know that I don't like to face fear, sadness or hurt (scared of being scared), and that won't change overnight. So I am trying to create two new habits that don't require constant vigilance. The first is a habit of approaching food with mindfulness of portions and nutrition, and not eating secretly. That is not so difficult, but it requires a second habit, and this is the hard one: learn how to respond to fear or hurt. For me, this second habit involves being mindful of my hurt by checking in, breathing and talking to people close to me. I need to continue to find new habits to increase my awareness and manage my sadness."

You may always need to be vigilant about what your body is asking for and how to feed it. This may not be easy. That is why we need a smorgasbord of tools to choose from to keep us on our path, to help us stop and think and to soothe in order to create a space before we act.

One Day at a Time

One day at a time is the Alcoholics Anonymous slogan because it works. Worrying about how much you will weigh by Aunt Margaret's second wedding in June creates unnecessary stress. When we are trying to beat an addiction we need to decrease stress wherever possible. Ending an addiction is a day-by-day process that takes the time it takes. Nothing can change that reality. Thinking long term pulls us out of the moment, into the mythical future where anxiety feeds. Repeating and formalizing this mantra by making it into a daily prayer will remind us that this is a journey, and like all journeys they happen one moment followed by another.

Start the day: 'Thank you for this day, help me be awake with my eating and nourish my body with love'.

End the day: 'Thank you for this day, and for my ability to choose what my body needed for its nourishment'.

Or simply say 'One day at a time'. When you awaken, and when you go to bed.

Do whatever reminds you that this change will happen one day at a time.

Find a Group or a Buddy

Over and over again research has shown that in order to make a permanent change, to successfully beat an addiction, we need community. We are not nearly as successful when we go it alone. Beating addiction is just too hard. Going it alone is about shame and our ego. I don't need help, its nobody's business, I can beat this thing. Statistically, you can't. So find a program, Overeaters Anonymous, or a twelve-step program designed for food addiction if you have one in your community and it feels right or find a trusted friend. That may be all you need, someone to talk to, share your struggles with. You and your friend can create what works for you as a team: a daily check in, emergency phone calls to help stop a binge, weekly success stories, etc. Put parameters around the subject so that it does not monopolize the conversation. If you walk with that friend daily, decide on an amount of time to limit the conversation. A parameter ensures that it stays productive, and shows that you are working toward ending the obsession around food, dieting, weight loss and all things related. Then, talk about something else.

Therapist

Ending food addiction is a tremendous challenge; it can open up many wounds, some deeply buried. Support from a professional may be imperative to help you stay on track, and help you with the trauma that lies beneath your addiction. Find a therapist who does somatic work (addresses what is going on in the body), who is able to help you find where your implicit memories live, where your traumas hide. There are numerous body centered therapeutic modalities available today and the therapists who use them are reporting great results in their quest to help people heal.

To end addiction you need to find ways to be with the emotions that pop up, ways to manage the uncovered traumas that present themselves. Once you take the lid off the can of worms it is really hard to slap it back on. So honor yourself by knowing when you need help and seek it out.

Mantras

Mantras are repetitive lines used as reminders or used to replace negative or obsessive thoughts. Write them down; put them in your journal, day-timer, on your wall, in your car, wherever you will come across them as tangible reminders. Create mantras that make sense and that you believe. Whenever you say a mantra take a deep breath with it so the words will flow into your body, not just your brain. The following are some suggestions.

➢ I can handle my emotions.
➢ I have everything I need.
➢ I have enough.
➢ I am enough.
➢ Everything is as it should be.
➢ I am learning.
➢ I am growing.
➢ I choose to love myself today.
➢ I choose to forgive myself today.
➢ I enjoy a wonderful, loving relationship with food.
➢ I choose to give my body what it needs in a loving way.

There are so many possible combinations, so pick one or create one that rings true to you. A mantra should resonate on a deep level for it to be effective. Some dismiss mantras as being fluffy or not useful. I have found the opposite. Using mantras is a way to make sure (again using the principles of the law of attraction) that you are telling yourself to attract to your life what you want. This counteracts negative vibrations that you may not even know you are sending out with your negative self-talk.

Along with breathing your mantra deeply into your body, it is repetition that counts. In his book *Outliers*, Malcolm Gladwell exposes the truth of why some people achieve such a high rate of success, why some people are the best at painting, writing, sports or business. In essence he debunks the popular notion that they are somehow special, or born that way, the prodigy theory. Malcolm shows, with fascinating evidence that successful people have enjoyed great opportunities, been lucky in fact, and have spent ten thousand hours engaged in their pursuit of choice. Ten thousand hours perfecting their craft![1] When you translate that to weight loss terms, my guess is you have spent way more than ten thousand hours telling yourself that you can't stop the overeating, you can't lose the weight, you will always be fat. Now it is time to tell yourself, repeatedly and with intent, something different. Powerful, not fluffy at all!

Tangible Reminders

Mala beads are a string of 108 beads with one large bead called a 'sumeru' or summit bead. These beads originate from ancient traditions, similar to the rosary beads used by Catholics for prayer. They are used as a tool for meditation. They help with concentration, counting them off while keeping time with your mantra and breath. Mine reside in my purse, then come out mid-afternoon, when I get home from work, before and after dinner. They are wrapped around my wrist most evenings or sitting somewhere close by. I use them during my identified trigger times, as tangible reminders to not eat mindlessly. Before I discovered this tool I would find myself, head in fridge, stuffing something into my mouth without noticing. It would be later—maybe only minutes later—that I would think, did I just eat that? Why? What are you doing?

The beads are like the reminder string around the finger, or elastic around the wrist. I appreciate the spiritual aspect to the beads because they remind me that the journey to end addiction is a spiritual journey. A journey to be more fully awake in the world.

Pick a tangible reminder that has significance to you, a stone you carry in your pocket, any talisman that has meaning, and keep it handy within your sight or on your person to help you through your trigger times.

Create a Safe Place

Spend some time in your imagination creating a beautiful place. This place may be one you have visited or one you imagine. Create a place that feels safe and serene, a place that fills you with peace. Engage all your senses. I envision a deck at the back of a house, nestled in the trees, part way up a hill from the ocean, surrounded by an old growth forest. I am relaxed, sitting in a chair, face lifted to the sun. The sun filtered by the trees warms me perfectly; I hear the rustle of the wind harmonize with the sound of the waves and the occasional cry of a gull. I catch the odd buzz of a humming bird and whiff of pine and the sea. I could stay there all day. This image fills me with warmth. I have visited it numerous times in my mind. It feels real to me. Once you have created your image, go there when your thoughts turn to food. Spend some time. When you feel rested, re-enter the world, fortified against your yearnings. If you decide you truly are hungry for food, you are now able to make decisions from a grounded, calm place.

The safe place you create is yours. It does not have to feel like you are at a spa. Some people envision themselves, dancing, sweating to an animal beat, wild and free. If that is the image of yourself that takes you away from your obsession about food, go for it.

The One-Minute Rule

Give yourself a one-minute rule: You're sitting, watching TV. You notice your thoughts turn to popcorn and pop. Excuse yourself, find a quiet place and breath for one minute then ask your body 'do I really want this'? If one minute does not seem enough, sit longer. If you find you are not hungry, congratulate yourself for interrupting your patterns. When you realize it is not food you crave, go to your safe image, say your mantras, or do a little meditating. Then pick up your talisman and carry on. Or go do something else; take a bath, go to bed or phone your buddy.

Tonglen

Tonglen is a Tibetan word that means sending and taking. The practice is designed to consciously invite our thoughts and feelings in, notice them, then let them go. Bring forth the thoughts and emotions we deem negative, are afraid of. Notice, then release. Expose them for what they are, just thoughts and emotions.

With anxiety, we tend to do the opposite. We don't notice the thoughts or feeling, and if we do, we add to our anxiety by saying more damaging, dead-end statements that consequently make the emotion harder to handle.

So again, find a quiet spot and sit. Label the emotion: 'guilt'. Get comfortable, breath deeply, then start the practice by saying 'I breathe in guilt' and let yourself feel the quality of that, where it lives in the body. Imagine hot, humid jungle air. Then pick an opposite word. Whatever feels right to you; 'peace'; 'I breathe out peace'. Imagine breathing out cool, crisp mountain air; surround yourself in it, visualize yourself in a bubble. Repeat this practice. 'I breathe in guilt, I breathe out peace'. The point of breathing in the guilt is to really notice it. You are training to be fearless. Fear is just a feeling. The practice of tonglen gives us a tool to shift our feelings and let go what we are carrying in that moment. Release it from our body. This practice gives us another way to manage our emotions instead of reaching for food.

Reminders

- ➤ Eat slowly; keep timing yourself until eating slowly is a habit.
- ➤ Eat with no distractions.
- ➤ Take smaller portions—practice eating less.
- ➤ Plan for your trigger times.
- ➤ Meditate daily in whatever form that takes.
- ➤ Have your reminders, tangible and tactile, handy for your trigger times.

- ➤ Do something else—paint, write, knit, sew, carve, clean, exercise.
- ➤ Learn something new.
- ➤ Keep noticing your breath—notice your stress levels.
- ➤ Take body breaks. Check in, whatever that looks like for you.
- ➤ Get a buddy.

Do Something Else

Addictions are time consuming. When you change your relationship with food you lose the obsession. You may find yourself not spending as much time planning meals, dreaming about food, reading cook books or watching cooking shows when food is no longer center stage. What are you going to do with all that free headspace, that free time? This could be the opportunity to embark upon one of those things you always wanted to do.

I've always wanted to learn to play the guitar; I've always wanted to paint; I would love to write poetry; wouldn't it be nice to plant a garden.

So do it!

I never have time to read; I never seem to have enough time for friends; I don't have time to exercise; I never have time to just be, sit quietly and rest.

Yes you do!

Getting passionate about something takes you to another place, one that is challenging, exciting and can bring out the best in you. It will make you feel alive!

Mike relates what guitar playing means to him, "Playing my guitar and making music was important as a means of self-soothing from the time I was fifteen. I set down the guitar at twenty-one and in doing so I lost an important non-food means of self-comfort. That increased my reliance on food and drink. After twenty-five years I have rediscovered the guitar. When I'm self-soothing, I play a largely formless blues, completely improvised, just as I did when I was a teenager, and it helps quite a bit. It is very different from when I'm practicing the guitar to increase skills, learn new songs, or rehearse for performing. Any time I'm playing guitar I'm not hungry or thinking about drinking. But when I'm improvising, it feels in some way like speaking directly to my sadness. At the same time, although I feel sadness, I remain present instead of in the 'suspended avoidance and unawareness with a mouth-full-of-food' state." Creativity soothes our soul.

Find something you love. I love cooking. Ending food addiction does not mean ending a love of cooking and eating. One of my absolute favorite days happens each fall, when I start nesting. I crank the tunes, have the kitchen laden with fall produce and do a great big cook off: squash soups, minestrone soup, chilis, stews, apple crisps, and baked apples. Fantastic. I am so happy in that place, the food addict is nowhere in sight, I am not shoveling or stuffing; I am not anxious, looking for a hit. I am grounded, relaxed, in the moment and truly me. I hope you know by now that addictive eating is not about loving food.

This has been a long process for me. I have been peeling back the layers, looking for clues of the 'why' behind my addictive eating for years, trying to find a way to lose weight and keep it off.

I still struggle, yet I have many more successes. I am now better at hearing what my body wants. I am better at discerning what I am hungry for: food, love, attention, acceptance, acknowledgment, stimulation, comfort and so much more. I try not to jump at first signal. Instead I sit with it, spend time with it, and be present with it. Sometimes there is nothing to be done and sometimes there is.

We all need to be present in our lives, which means showing up and paying attention. We must speak our truth, sometimes out loud, but always in our minds. The results will be the results. In our result driven society it is difficult to just sit with that, especially when we want to lose weight. But it is far more likely that it will happen if we follow the first steps. When we are awake to ourselves, we can't hide the fact that the second piece of pie is about feeding our emotion and not our bodies. If we show up and pay attention, the moment comes into focus. We can see it for what it is and make conscious choices. The truth of the moment is revealed, what we need is noted. When we stop obsessing about the outcome, let it go and learn to trust, turn toward our emotions with kindness and compassion, something magical happens. We learn to feed ourselves with love instead of food.

JOURNALING

THERE ARE SO many ways to write in a journal. For therapeutic purposes, I suggest you don't look at your journal so much in terms of a diary, writing in the mundane aspects of each day, but use it as a place to follow the threads of your thoughts you deem relevant to the process of ending your food addiction. This is a place to expose them on paper, see what you written and attempt to make sense of them.

Cart your journal around with you, have it handy, put it in a place where you notice it. This book is your friend, a place to tap into your inner wisdom. You can create daily questions; create a format to follow such as in the two weeks suggested in chapter five to track specifically what you eat, and what your trigger times are. The journal can be used to do the three questions posed in chapter eight, three times daily; how do I feel? What is that? What do I need?

Use your journal to debrief a binge; find the why, the route you took that led to the binge by breaking it down. Find the pivotal point (if there was one) where you could have stopped the behavior, turned a corner and did something different. Why didn't you? Get curious and stay compassionate.

Your journal should be fun. Add inspirational quotes, mantras, nuggets that lift you and give you hope. Paste in feathers, pictures; make it special, a place you want to spend time. If you prefer to use your computer, go ahead, just commit to the process. Enjoy it and use it as tangible reminder that you are learning to honor yourself.

ACKNOWLEDGMENTS

First and foremost I want to thank the members of the Vicious Circle Writers Group, the best critique group on the planet. The truth is without these ladies, Rebecca Wood Barrett, Katherine Fawcett, Stella Harvey, Sara Leach, Mary MacDonald, Libby McKeever and Sue Oakey this book would never have been finished.

Thanks go to the talented writers Merilyn Simonds and Wayne Grady. They generously imparted their knowledge and expertise and inspired me to believe in the work and myself.

A thank you to my friends and family who were behind me, listened to my ideas and provided insightful feedback: Donna, Brenda, LeeAnn, Sandy, Jill, Chris, Bry and of course my son Will and his love Shani, and my daughter Heidi and her love Luke. I have wonderful people in my life who champion all my endeavors with genuine enthusiasm.

A special thanks to those who contributed their stories, 'Julie, Linda, Mike and Darlene.' You know who you are. Good luck and keep going forward in your quest to feed yourself love.

Thanks to my editor Julie Malcolm, for your thoughtful critique and support. I am so fortunate to have found you at the eleventh hour.

Warm thanks to master therapists Bob Finlay and Brenda Montani, for taking the time to read my manuscript and provide invaluable insights and a therapist point of view.

To my parents, thanks for reading over the parts about my childhood and remaining my biggest fans. And yes I will 'suck it up!'

And lastly, a thank you to my husband Tony. Although you have an annoying habit of interrupting me when I am trying to write, I know you are always 100% behind me. Never in our thirty-five years together have you said a critical word about my weight struggles. That means so much to me.

ABOUT THE AUTHOR

NANCY ROUTLEY IS a fifty-some married woman who has been working and living Whistler, B.C. since 1993. She is a psychotherapist in private practice, a profession she is very passionate about.

She writes and paints, loves the outdoors and purses many sports such as hiking, biking and skiing. These endeavors seem pretty impressive to her friends in other places in the world, but as she explains she can barely keep up to the Whistler fifty plus mamas she hangs with!

In recent years Nancy has found herself devoting more time to writing, feeling compelled to write about what moves her, commentaries on life, basically why it is we do what we do. She also dabbles at fiction.

ENDNOTES

L. Lansens, *A Wife's Tale* (Vintage Canada, A Division of Random House, 2009, Little Brown and Company)

Intro
1. P. Kennar, *I Can Make You Thin* (Sterling Publishing Company, New York, 2009), 10
2. E. Tribole & E. Resch, Intuitive Eating, A Recovery Book for the Chronic Dieter, Rediscover the Pleasures of Eating and Rebuild Your Body Image (St. Martin's Press, New York, 1995) 76

Chapter One—Addictions
1. P. Kennar, *I Can Make You Thin* (Sterling Publishing Company, New York, 2009), 10
2. G. Mate, *In The Realm of Hungry Ghosts* (Alfred A. Knopf Canada, 2008), 128

3. C. Northrup, *The Wisdom of Menopause* (Bantam Books, 2001), 197

4. E. Tolle, *A New Earth, Awakening to Your Life's Purpose* (Plume, Penguin Group,2005), 246

5. G. Mate, *In The Realm of Hungry Ghosts* (Alfred A. Knopf Canada, 2008), 168

6. G. Mate, *In The Realm of Hungry Ghosts* (Alfred A. Knopf Canada, 2008), 290

Chapter Three—Hunger By Any Other Name

1. G. Mate, *In The Realm of Hungry Ghosts* (Alfred A. Knopf Canada, 2008), 220

2. C. Northrup, *The Wisdom of Menopause* (Bantam Books, 2001), 197

3. J. Goldstein, *Abiding in Mindfulness, On Feelings, The Mind & Dhamma* , CD, Sounds True Inc. Boulder CO, 2007

4. G. Mate, *In The Realm of Hungry Ghosts* (Alfred A. Knopf Canada, 2008), 232

5. G. Roth, *When Food Is Love* (Plume, Penguin Group, 1992), 117

Chapter Four—Stop the World, I Want to Get Off

J. Kabat-Zinn, Full Catastrophe Living, (Bantam Dell, A Division of Random House, Inc. New York, 1990) XXXII

Chapter Five – What the Hell am I Supposed to Eat

1. P. Kennar, *I Can Make You Thin* (Sterling Publishing Company, New York, 2009), 11

2. J Beck, *The Beck Diet Solution Weight Loss Workbook* (Oxmoor House Inc. USA, 2007) 69

3. E. Tribole & E. Resch, *Intuitive Eating, A Recovery Book for the Chronic Dieter, Rediscover the Pleasures of Eating and Rebuild Your Body Image* (St. Martin's Press, New York, 1995) 128

4. L. Neporent, *Out of Control Portion Sizes,* (http://www.thatsfit.com/2009/05/29/out-of-control-portion-sizes)

5. G. Roth, *When Food Is Love* (Plume, Penguin Group, 1992), 117

Chapter Six – You Gotta To Move It Move It

1. Anonymous, *200 Ways to Love the Body You Have,* (http://www.bodypositive.com) 5

2. Kate Lunau, *All The Right Moves,* (Maclean's Magazine, Volume 123 Number 18, May 17, 2010) 48

3. J. Cloud, *Why Exercise Won't Make You Thin,* (Time Magazine, August 17, 2009) 49

4. J. Cloud, *Why Exercise Won't Make You Thin,* (Time Magazine, August 17, 2009) 46(check)

5. J. Cloud, *Why Exercise Won't Make You Thin,* (Time Magazine, August 17, 2009) 47

Chapter Seven—The spiritual Realm

1. *http://en.wikipedia.org/wiki/Obesity_in_the_United_States*

2. E. Tolle, *A New Earth, Awakening to Your Life's Purpose* (Plume, Penguin Group, 2005), 18

Chapter Eight—The Mindful Way Home

1. P. Chodron, *The Wisdom of No Escape and the Path of Loving Kindness*, (Shambhala Publications, Inc., USA, 1991) 14
2. E. Tolle, *A New Earth, Awakening to Your Life's Purpose* (Plume, Penguin Group,2005), 27
3. E. Tolle, *A New Earth, Awakening to Your Life's Purpose* (Plume, Penguin Group,2005), 78
4. D. Simon & D. Chopra, *Freedom From Addiction* (Health Communications, Inc. 2007) 60
5. D. Siegel, *Mindsight, The New Science of Personal Transformation* (Bantam Books, Division of Random House, New York, 2010), 86
6. D. Simon & D. Chopra, *Freedom From Addiction* (Health Communications, Inc. 2007) 72
7. P. Chodron, *The Wisdom of No Escape and the Path of Loving Kindness*, (Shambhala Publications, Inc., USA, 1991) 95

Chapter Nine—It Takes a Smorgasbord to Beat An Addiction

1. M. Gladwell, *Outliers – the Story of Success* (Hachette Book Group, 2008), 40